STAGES, TRANSPORTATION.

A. N. FISHER & Co.'s
1856.
LINE OF STAGES,
FOR SONORA, COLUMBIA
Jamestown, Montezuma, Chinese Camp, Mound Springs, Green Springs, Knight's Ferry, Mokelumne Hill, Campo Seco & Double Springs;

Mariposa, Agua Frio, Mount Ophir, Quartzburg, Hornitis, Snelling's Ranch, Young's, Dickinson's, and Heath & Emory's Ferries.

MARIPOSA via FRENCH BAR, PLEASANT VALLEY, AND MERCED RIVER—PHILLIPS' FERRY.

—ALSO—

From MARIPOSA to SONORA and COLUMBIA via PLEASANT VALLEY, FRENCH BAR, COULTERSVILLE, MAXWELL'S CREEK, DON PEDRO'S BAR, AND MOUND SPRINGS.

☞ The above Lines leave Daily, at six o'clock A.M. Office corner Centre and Levee streets, in the old El Dorado building.

A. N. FISHER & CO.,
Proprietors.
P. B. MINTZER, Agent.

Dillon & Compny.
1856.
STAGES LEAVE THE COMPANY'S OFFICE.
Corner Centre st. and the Levee, Daily,
For Sonora, Columbia, Campo Seco, Mok. Hill, Murphy's,
AND ALL PARTS OF THE STATE.

---

of Wells, Fargo & Co.

SAN FRANCISCO, Oct. 15th, 1858.

Offices at VISALIA and FORT TEJON.

to San Francisco.

isco are as follows:

cents per pound.
  do and 1½ pr ct. on value.
, 20 cts. per pound.
  do. do. and 2 pr ct. on value.
, 32 cts. per pound and 2½ pr ct. do.

ed over $500 in value, to either of the Offices

SAMUEL KNIGHT,
Superintendent.

CHANGE OF TIME.

HORNITOS AND VISALIA STAGE LINE

On and after May 12th, 1868, Stages will leave Visalia every Tuesday, Thursday and Saturday, for Smith's Ferry, Centreville, Millerton, Fresno River, Buchanan Hollow, Mariposa Creek, Indian Gulch and Hornitos. Connecting with Fisher & Co.'s Stages from Stockton, at Hornitos, and with A. O. Thoms' Stages for Kernville and the Clear Creek Mines, at Visalia.

Returning.

Leaves HORNITOS on the same days until further notice.

May 12 tf P. BENNETT, Proprietor.

U. S. Mail Telegraph Stage Line.

FOR
Gilroy, Visalia, Tule River, Linn's Valley, Kern River, Havilah and Owen's River.

Leaves Gilroy and Visalia daily (Sundays excepted.) Leaves Gilroy on arrival of the morning train from San Francisco, connecting with stages to Millerton and Bakersfield.

	FARE.	TIME.
San Francisco to Visalia	$20	36 hours.
San Francisco to Havilah	$35	2 days.
San Francisco to Owens River	$50	4 days.

DIRECT FOR OWENS RIVER!

via Kahwea Trail. Stages leaves Visalia on Monday, Wednesday, and Friday, arriving at San Jose next day, in time for the 4 o'clock train for San Francisco.

Time from San Francisco to Visalia, 32 hours.
"   "   "   "   Kern River, 3 dys.
"   "   "   "   Owens " 4 days.

Passengers allowed 30 pounds of baggage.
This line has been restocked with the best quality of new coaches. For information apply to

W. G. ROBERTS, 208, Montgomery st. S. F.
J. KNOWLTON, Jr., Gilroy.
S. W. THOMS, Visalia.
A. A. BERMUDEZ, Havilah, Agents.
49-12tf.

STAGECOACH HEYDAY

Autographed for Jean Miller, with appreciation for the map-making artistry of Jim Miller

W. Harland Boyd
August 10, 1983
Bakersfield, California

STAGECOACH HEYDAY

IN THE SAN JOAQUIN VALLEY
1853-1876

by
William Harland Boyd

Kern County Historical Society, Inc.
Bakersfield, California
1983

To my wife,
Mary Kay

Copyright © 1983
by the Kern County Historical Society, Inc.
All rights reserved.

Manufactured in the United States of America.

Pioneer Publishing Company
Fresno, California 93728

ISBN 0-943500-10-9

Contents

Foreword   ix

Acknowledgements   xi

Chapter I   1
From the San Joaquin Valley to the Mines on the Stanislaus, Tuolumne and Merced Rivers

Chapter II   15
From Los Angeles to San Francisco by Way of Fort Tejon, Visalia, Gilroy and San Jose

Chapter III   25
From Visalia to Hornitos by Way of Scottsburg and Millerton

Chapter IV   35
From Visalia to San Jose by Way of Whitmore's and Firebaugh's Ferries and Gilroy

Chapter V   43
From Visalia to the Kern River Mines and Lone Pine and from Los Angeles

Chapter VI   51
From Advancing Railheads, Starting in the San Joaquin and San Fernando Valleys

Chapter VII   59
Stalking the Stages: The Holdup Men, Who Were Known as "Road Agents"

Bibliography   69

Index   71

Illustrations

Stockton in 1860	3
Sonora's Washington Street in about 1865	5
Mariposa in 1854	7
Main street of Hornitos	11
Phineas Banning	19
Millerton on the San Joaquin River in 1873	27
Amos O. Thoms	34
Visalia businesses in about 1864	37
Henry M. Newhall	39
Havilah, boom town of the 1860s	47
Bakersfield businesses in the 1870s	53
Silver bullion on the Mojave Desert in 1876	57
"Black Bart" (Charles E. Boles)	61
Tiburcio Vasquez	63
Wanted poster for Richard Perkins, alias G. Brett Lytle, alias Dick Fellow, alias Richard Kirtland	65

Maps

Stage routes in the Northern San Joaquin Valley, 1850-1876	xii
Stage routes in the Southern San Joaquin Valley, 1854-1876	17

Foreword

For nearly forty years William Harland Boyd has played a major role in promoting an understanding of the history of Kern County, its principal city of Bakersfield, and the southern San Joaquin Valley generally. Despite the demands of his teaching responsibilities as a professor at Bakersfield College and of his six-year chairmanship of that institution's social science department, he has nevertheless found time to help preserve the records of his region's past and to write books and articles that have made known some of the more striking personalities in Kern County's history. If my arithmetic is correct, the number of published volumes that Dr. Boyd has written or edited totals ten, and now comes still another. Quite aside from this impressive amount of authorship and editorship, Dr. Boyd has been active for many years in the Kern County Historical Society and more recently on the Kern County Historical Records Commission.

Truly this is an impressive example of service to the cause of history in one's home area. In the present volume he is returning to a theme that he discussed many years ago in an article published in the *Pacific Historical Review*. That article and, much more so, this well-organized little book do much to remedy what has been a neglect of San Joaquin Valley stagecoaching. The principal monograph on stagecoaching, Oscar Winther's *Express and Stagecoach Days in California*, has its focus on the gold rush era and on the heavily traveled regions north of Stockton. Through trying to cover a big subject in a small space, Winther's book left little room for areas such as the San Joaquin, despite the important travel through Stockton to the southern mines. Dr.

Boyd's new book, with its precise outlines of stagecoach ownership and operation, gives all its attention to the San Joaquin and covers the full quarter-century between the gold rush and the building of the Southern Pacific Railroad.

This was the pioneer era in Kern County's history. It was the period of the great California gold rush of 1848-1853 and of the ill-fated rush to the Kern River mines in 1855. It was the time of the great livestock ranches, of the spread southward of wheat, of the beginning of irrigation, and the founding of the first little towns and mercantile establishments. Somehow the people mixed up in these varied enterprises had to travel. It is their story that Dr. Boyd's new book helps to explain.

Rodman W. Paul

Pasadena
February 22, 1983

Acknowledgements

My thanks to the helpful staffs of the University of California's Bancroft Library at Berkeley, the California Section of the State Library at Sacramento, the Stockton Public Library at Stockton, the Stanislaus County Library at Modesto, the Merced County Library at Merced, the Fresno County Library at Fresno, the Tulare County Library at Visalia, and the Kern County Library at Bakersfield. Likewise, invaluable help was rendered by the staffs of the Clerks' and Recorders' offices of Tuolumne, Mariposa, Merced, Tulare and Kern counties.

Much appreciated, too, was the help of the individuals who shared information, supplied photographs, read the manuscript, etc.—Raymond W. Hillman of the Haggin Museum at Stockton; Carlo M. De Ferrari, Mary Etta Sagerstrom and Frank McCormick of the Tuolumne County Historical Society; Marian Thomson and Bertha Schroeder of the Mariposa County Historical Society; Harold Schutt, Annie Mitchell, Joseph Doctor, Merrill Goudie and Irene Turner of the Tulare County Historical Society; Jack Rump, Marjorie Rump and Curtis Darling of the Kern County Historical Society; Robert Merriam and Ardis Walker of Kern River Valley Historical Society.

My thanks, also, go to Mary Haas and Mary Hanel of the reference department of the Beale Branch of the Kern County Library; Vince Barry and John Ludeke of Bakersfield College, who read the manuscript; James Miller, who drafted the maps; Mary Kay Boyd, who helped type the manuscript; and Rodman W. Paul of the California Institute of Technology, who wrote the foreword. Helpful, too, were Will Dallons and his staff at the Sierra Graphic Center, designers of the title page, and G. Earl and Ellen Gray, who read the proofs.

W. Harland Boyd
Bakersfield, California
March 1, 1983

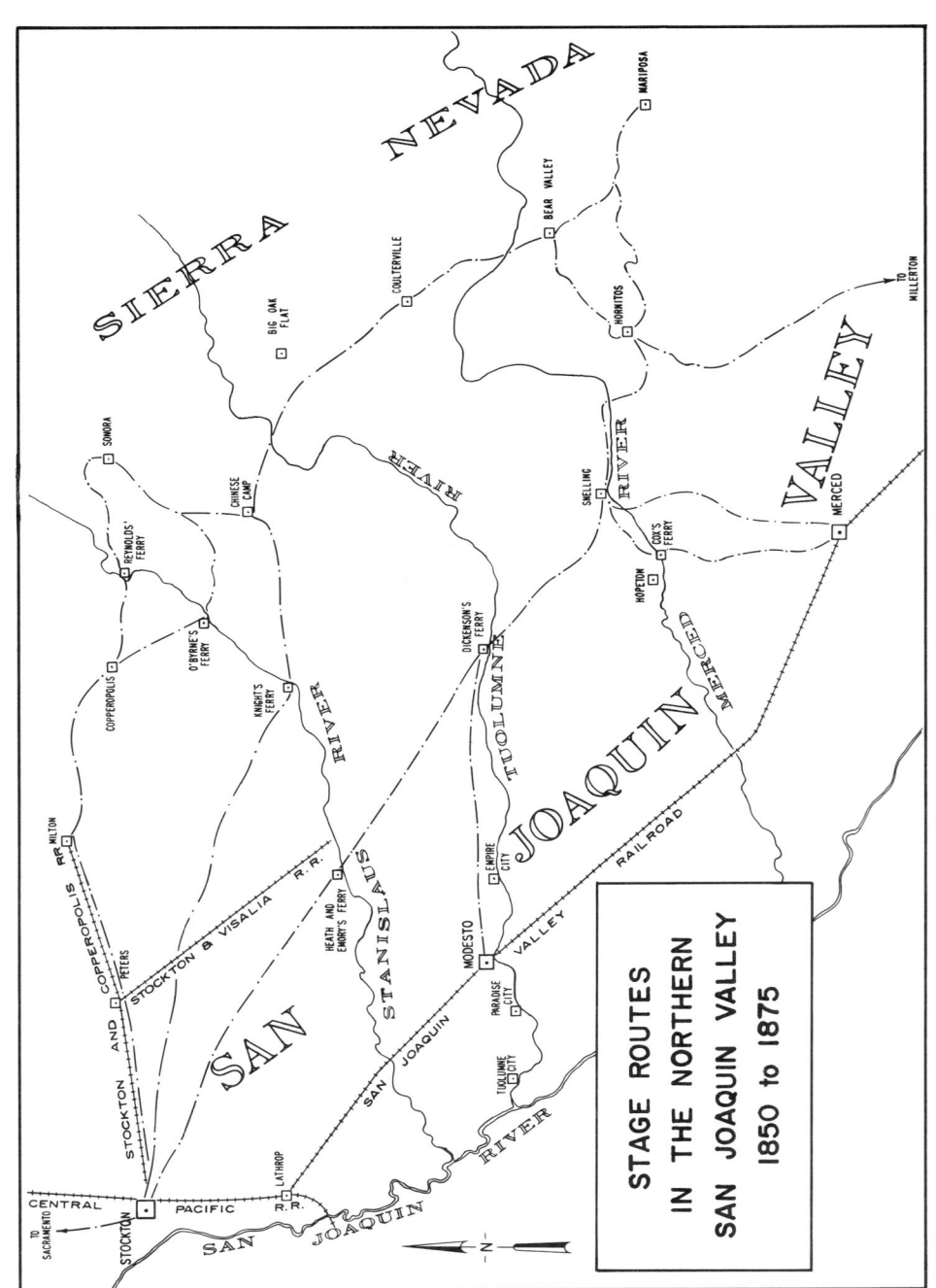

CHAPTER I

FROM THE SAN JOAQUIN VALLEY TO THE MINES ON THE STANISLAUS, TUOLUMNE, AND MERCED RIVERS 1853-1874

*"To those who have taken this ride we offer...
sympathy, and to those who have not... if you
wish to know of what you are made, try it."*
—Mariposa Gazette, June 17, 1870

STARTING WITH the gold rush to California in the spring of 1849, Stockton was a busy San Joaquin River port. During the gold excitement, according to a newspaperman, ten or twelve daily stages ran between the wharf and the mines in the Sierra Nevada.[1] Some stagemen were in business for only a few months, while others continued for several years. Their rolling stock ranged from ordinary buggies or wagons, pulled by mustang horses, to fine coaches, drawn by blooded animals. Not only did they compete for passengers, but there was rivalry as well for the mail and express. While the stagemen engaged in "rate wars" in their efforts to attract patronage and eliminate competitors, the drivers sometimes tried to outdistance each other as they raced along the roadways.

From Stockton the stage drivers went as speedily "as on any other stage roads." One rider noted that when "the coaches came down the hills and over the plains a whizzing," the excitement was exhilarating.[2] Some left the town by way of the Sonora Road, which went southeast to Knight's Ferry on the Stanislaus River. After a climb to Chinese Camp, the road turned north through Montezuma and Jamestown to Sonora, some seventy miles from Stockton. Other stages went southeast by way of the Mariposa Road to Heath and Emory's Ferry on the Stanislaus, Dickenson's Ferry on the Tuolumne, and Snelling, a "leafy oasis," on the Merced River. From upriver Merced Falls, the road turned southeast to Hornitos and east to Mariposa, although by late 1857, if not earlier, stages were going less directly by way of the Bear Valley Road. Beyond a northeast climb to Bear Valley the drivers turned southeast to Mariposa, some ninety miles from Stockton.

Characterizing Stockton's stage proprietors as "all liberal, energetic men," the *San Joaquin Republican* in July, 1854, stated that they deserved "a full tide of prosperity." Their firms were well patronized, and this was especially the case with those in business on the Sonora Road.[3] Mentioned particularly were proprietors Alvin N. Fisher and his brother Samuel Fisher and Eugene Kelty and his associate Gilbert C. Reynolds. Their horses were "of the noblest breeds," and their coaches were Concords.[4] Another stage proprietor active on the Sonora Road was Alonzo McCloud, who owned the Red Bird Line.[5]

The California Stage Company, under the presidency of James E. Birch, consolidated many northern California stage firms in January, 1854. Still others were absorbed in December, including most companies operating on the Sonora Road.[6] Making known their "opposition to monopoly," Alvin N. and Samuel Fisher, after acquiring Alonzo McCloud's stages, formed A. N. Fisher and Company, which in January, 1855, began to run in competition with the California Stage Company.[7] The latter company, after operating for a year without a mail contract, withdrew from the Sonora Road in January, 1856. Its stock and stages were sold to John Dillon and Maurice J. Dooley, who comprised Dillon and Company.[8]

Stockton in 1860. (From Hutchings' *California Magazine*, February, 1860.)

Their firm competed with A. N. Fisher and Company, and in May another stage company was organized by, among others, Eugene Kelty and Gilbert C. Reynolds.[9] The rival fares were so drastically reduced that the *San Joaquin Republican* urged all who liked to travel to "embrace the ... opportunity." Many heeded the advice. Indeed, during a single day in July, 168 riders from various mining towns reached Stockton.[10]

During the palmy gold rush years the mining activities along the Tuolumne, Stanislaus and Merced rivers generated enough passenger, mail and express business to support several stage companies. Yet by the mid-1850s the placer mining was playing out, and the developing quartz or hard rock mining was costly and afforded less employment. As flush times yielded to dull times in the late 1850s, the mining population decreased.[11] Sonora's economy was declining when, in December, 1860, Dillon and Company became M. J. Dooley and Company.[12] In August, 1861, at a time of worsening economic conditions, A. N. Fisher and Company ceased to operate to Sonora.[13]

The disruptive Civil War had been over for more than a year when, through a stage notice in the *Sacramento Union* in August, 1866, James A. Ellison, who lived north of Stockton on the Mokelumne River, advertised the successful operation of his stages linking Sacramento, Stockton, Sonora and Mariposa.[14] Not only was Ellison awarded the mail contract formerly held by M. J. Dooley and Company, but he also competed with that firm for passengers on the Sonora Road. Sonorans welcomed the opposition in the hope that lower fares and speedier service would result.[15] In November a Dooley driver, Samuel Brown, arrived well ahead of schedule at Sonora, thereby inspiring a newspaperman to announce that he always patronized "the fast line," for it was nothing to him "if horse flesh ... suffer[ed]."[16]

When Ellison's contract for the carrying of mail be-

Sonora's Washington Street in about 1865. (Courtesy, Mary Etta Sagerstrom)

tween Stockton and Sonora was renewed in the spring of 1867, less compensation was allowed for the service. In August the *Sonora Herald* reported that Ellison had been "froze[n] out by the extensive stage owners, Messrs. Dooley and Company." Subsequently the latter firm curtailed its services, claiming that the patronage was declining and many travelers were driving hired conveyances between Stockton and Sonora.[17] In September M. J. Dooley and Company was acquired by Charles A. Sisson.[18]

In May, 1870, the People's Accommodation and Express Company, with sponsors at Stockton, Knight's Ferry, Chinese Camp and Sonora, was organized in the hope of reducing the stage fares. In June the inaugural stage left Stockton with a full load.[19] Vowing to spend money for "defense" but not for "blackmail," C. H. Sisson and Company drastically reduced its fares.[20] These reductions prevailed until the rains were at hand and the "citizens' line" suspended operations in October. Although the sponsors expected to resume business the following summer, the firm was dissolved in June, 1871. C. H. Sisson and Company was charging only moderate fares, and the *Union Democrat* explained that the citizenry had forgotten the "old scores."[21]

In September, 1869, the Central Pacific Railroad linked Sacramento and San Francisco Bay by way of Stockton, and construction began on the San Joaquin Valley Railroad at Lathrop in December.[22] When the Stockton and Copperopolis Railroad began operations to Peters in February, 1871, the *San Joaquin Republican* observed that railroads extended in all directions from Stockton.[23] The last outclassed stage firm to retreat from the town was C. H. Sisson and Company, which first connected with the railroad at Peters and then at Milton, where construction ceased in May.[24] From the railhead the Sonora-bound stages went by way of Copperopolis to a

Mariposa in 1854. (Courtesy, Mariposa Photographic Reproductions)

crossing of the Stanislaus River at either Reynolds' or O'Byrne's ferries.

Long after the gold rush was over in the Sierra Nevada, the stage patronage was generated mostly by the mining activities. Yet by the late 1860s a substantial number of summer tourists visited the Calaveras Grove and the Yosemite Valley. These popular resorts, one to the north and one to the southeast of Sonora, were about eighty miles apart by way of that town.[25] The *Sonora Democrat* urged visitors to enjoy the beauty of the Calaveras Grove before the grandeur of the Yosemite Valley.[26] Until roads were opened to the latter in the mid-1870s, the tourists completed their journey on horseback. Vying businessmen lured them by way of Big Oak Flat, Coulterville and Mariposa. After the Central Pacific Railroad was completed to a transcontinental connection in May, 1869, more than eleven hundred summer sightseers reportedly went to the Yosemite Valley, a majority of whom came from outside California.[27]

A. N. Fisher and Company had run stages on both the Sonora and Mariposa roads until August, 1861, but at that time the *Stockton Independent* listed it solely as a "Mariposa Line."[28] For nearly two decades A. N. Fisher and Company, S. and Z. Fisher's Stage Line and Fisher and Company dominated the staging on the Mariposa Road. Yet James A. Ellison, who extended his widespread stage operations to the Sonora Road in August, 1866, at the same time put mail-carrying stages on the Mariposa Road.[29] After A. N. Fisher and Company lowered its fares, the *Mariposa Gazette* reported that its stages carried full loads, while those of the newcomer were virtually without passengers.[30] Whips were freely used when contending drivers raced between Bear Valley and Hornitos, and the Fishers' driver easily won the contest.[31] Ellison made a gallant but unsuccessful effort to compete until his line "unexpectedly collapsed" in January, 1867, and A. N. Fisher and Company again carried the mail between Stockton and Mariposa.[32] Although Alvin N. Fisher had died in November, 1863, the stage company continued to bear his name until March, 1868, when his brothers, Samuel and Zenas, renamed it S. and Z. Fisher's Stage Line.[33]

While most of the San Joaquin Valley remained a cattle domain, by the late 1860s farmers were settling on the plains south of Stockton. In June, 1868, S. and Z. Fisher's Stage Line provided stage services to Tuolumne City and Paradise City on the Tuolumne River.[34] At first the proprietors were without a mail contract, but they voluntarily made deliveries, for which they were compensated by the "contributions of a few public spirited citizens." Subsequently they were awarded a contract to carry the mail as far as Paradise City, some thirty-five miles southeast of Stockton.[35]

In July, 1870, Lemuel H. Silman was granted a contract to carry the mail between Stockton and Millerton, and he routed his stages by way of Tuolumne City and Paradise City, as well as Snelling on the Merced River. At the last minute he was authorized to carry the mail onward to Visalia.[36] The *Tuolumne City News* expressed satisfaction with the routing of the stages but disappointment with only weekly mail deliveries.[37] That same complaint was expressed at Millerton, where some residents regarded Silman's firm as "an outrageous humbug." They hoped for its collapse and the restoration of previously satisfactory mail service by way of Hornitos.[38]

S. and Z. Fisher's Stage Line became more competitive with that of Silman in August, 1870, when the proprietors extended their Tuolumne River line beyond Paradise City to Snelling.[39] In October a Silman associate began to operate an opposition line between Snelling and Mariposa, and this precipitated a rate war with S. and Z. Fisher's Stage Line. In December, in what the *Mariposa Gazette* reported to be an "entirely voluntary" move on his part, all stage operations were suspended by Silman.[40]

In December, 1870, a year after southbound construction was undertaken on the San Joaquin Valley Railroad at Lathrop, the railhead was at Modesto, and S. and Z. Fisher's Stage Line began to dispatch its Mariposa-bound stages from the new railroad town on the Tuolumne River.[41] Thirteen months later, in January, 1872, railroad construction reached Merced, and the Mariposa-bound stages were routed northward over the Snelling Road. When high water made it hazardous to ford the Merced River, the drivers crossed downstream at Cox's Ferry.[42] While S. and Z. Fisher's Stage Line was operating from Merced, Zenas Fisher died in May, 1872. Samuel Fisher, using the name Fisher and Company, became the sole proprietor. He died in April, 1874.[43]

The roads over which the stages traveled were dusty in summer, muddy in winter. One stormy day in February, 1857, the *San Joaquin Republican* reported that no stages left Stockton, and only one arrived from Sonora. That stage had been on the road for two days.[44] When heavy rains stalled a stage at Hornitos in February, 1862, an accommodating driver carried the mail on horseback to Mariposa.[45] In January, 1867, some stage horses became mired in mud near Knight's Ferry; one died before it could be rescued.[46] When the stages were operating from Merced in January, 1873, the town was surrounded by a sea of mud, and only with the help of a farmer's team could a driver move his vehicle along a six-mile stretch of road.[47]

As careful as the stage drivers were, accidents occasionally occurred on the Sonora and Mariposa roads. Wesley B. Dowst was crossing the plains southwest of Stockton in February, 1865, when he was thrown from his seat and run over by the stage. Severely injured, he remained to recuperate on the Stanislaus River.[48] In January, 1867, "Old Honesty" (T. N.) Gardner was loading

Main Street of Hornitos. (Courtesy, Mariposa Photographic Reproductions)

baggage when the horses "took fright" at Chinese Camp. He was unable to restrain them, and a passenger was bruised when the careening vehicle overturned.[49] In July Charles Morse's stage struck a boulder near Rock River House, and he was thrown between the wheel horses. Gaining their freedom when the stage was upset, the startled animals ran away. Morse was slightly injured, and a passenger was bruised.[50] "Old Honesty" Gardner's stage toppled in September between Chinese Camp and Knight's Ferry, injuring the passengers. Describing "Old Honesty" as a "most careful driver," the *Sonora Herald* blamed the accident on the agent who overloaded the stage.[51]

In September, 1873, Peter Gordon's stage was involved in an accident near Mariposa Creek. Although Gordon was a careful reinsman, all aboard the stage found themselves "fearfully and wonderfully mixed with dust and rocks." Indeed, some of the passengers were severely injured.[52] When Simeon H. Mott's stage was approaching Hornitos in October, 1873, a pedestrian frightened the horses, and they became unmanageable. The stage was smashed against a building, slightly injuring the sole passenger.[53]

Typically, a crowd gathered at the interior towns such as Sonora and Mariposa to meet the stages bearing passengers, mail, express and newspapers. For a week in February, 1869, rains disrupted travel to Mariposa, and when a stage finally arrived the greeters threw hats into the air, waved handkerchiefs and shouted huzzas.[54] For a few years the Fishers used Concord stages between Stockton and Hornitos, while less commodious vehicles were sent over the mountains to Mariposa. When James L. Snediker, a "prince of Jehus," drove a Concord stage to that town in May, 1869, the *Mariposa Gazette* reported that he looked like "Neptune upon the bow of a Clipper."[55] One evening in January, 1874, the townsmen heard the echoed cry of "Stage!" and the "genuine rattle of wheels."

But it turned out to be only an old wagon pulled at a trot by some jokesters.[56]

When in February, 1871, the railroad competition forced the last stage company to retreat from Stockton, the editor of the *San Joaquin Republican* recalled the time when "stages left every morning for all parts of the southern and middle mines, and for towns and villages in the north and south." Now instead of riding in crowded stages pulled by "smoking horses," travelers were luxuriating in coaches pulled by "iron horses." Yet the editor recognized the inevitable change that comes with "enterprise and progress."[57]

NOTES

1. *San Joaquin Republican*, December 17, 1851.
2. Ibid., October 23, 1854.
3. Ibid., July 15, 1854.
4. Ibid., June 28, 1853.
5. Ibid., September 13, 1853.
6. Ibid., December 13, 15, 1854; Oscar O. Winther, *Via Western Express and Stagecoach*, 10-11.
7. *San Joaquin Republican*, January 6, 1855; George H. Tinkham, *History of San Joaquin County, California*, 103.
8. *San Joaquin Republican*, January 12, 15, 1856.
9. Ibid., May 16, 1856.
10. Ibid., May 16, July 3, 1856.
11. Rodman W. Paul, *California Gold: The Beginning of Mining in the Far West*, 240; *A History of Tuolumne County, California*, 233-34.
12. *San Joaquin Republican*, December 13, 14, 1860.
13. *Stockton Independent*, August 1, 1861.
14. *Sacramento Union*, August 3, 1866.
15. *Union Democrat*, July 7, 1866.
16. Ibid., November 17, 1866.
17. *Sonora Herald*, August 29, 1867.
18. *Union Democrat*, September 28, October 5, 1867.
19. Ibid., June 11, 1870.
20. *San Joaquin Republican*, June 7, 1870.
21. *Union Democrat*, November 5, 1870, May 13, June 24, 1871.

22. *Sacramento Union*, September 7, 8, 1869; *Southern Pacific Bulletin*, August, 1955, 18.
23. *San Joaquin Republican*, February 22, 1871.
24. *Union Democrat*, February 25, May 27, 1871.
25. *Ibid.*, July 3, 1869.
26. *Ibid.*, June 14, 1873.
27. *Stockton Independent*, April 13, 1870.
28. *Ibid.*, August 1, 1861.
29. *Mariposa Gazette*, July 7, 1866.
30. *Ibid.*, July 14, 1866.
31. *Ibid.*, July 28, 1866.
32. *Ibid.*, January 26, 1867.
33. *Stockton Independent*, November 23, 1863; *Mariposa Gazette*, March 14, 1868.
34. *Stockton Independent*, June 13, 1868.
35. *Tuolumne City News*, July 1, 1870.
36. *Ibid.*; *Visalia Delta*, August 3, 1870.
37. *Tuolumne City News*, July 1, 1870.
38. *Fresno Expositor*, November 30, 1870.
39. *Tuolumne City News*, August 12, 1870.
40. *Ibid.*, October 14, 1870; *Mariposa Gazette*, October 7, December 9, 23, 1870.
41. *Mariposa Gazette*, December 16, 1870.
42. *Ibid.*, February 9, 1872, January 23, 1874.
43. *Stockton Independent*, May 24, 1872, April 23, 1874; *Mariposa Gazette*, July 3, 1874.
44. *San Joaquin Republican*, February 19, 1857.
45. *Ibid.*, February 5, 1862.
46. *Sonora Herald*, January 19, 1867.
47. *Mariposa Gazette*, January 3, 1873.
48. *Ibid.*, February 25, 1865.
49. *Sonora Herald*, January 5, 1867.
50. *Union Democrat*, July 13, 1867.
51. *Sonora Herald*, September 14, 1867.
52. *Mariposa Gazette*, September 12, 1873.
53. *Ibid.*, October 24, 1873.
54. *Ibid.*, February 19, 1869.
55. *Ibid.*, May 27, 1859.
56. *Ibid.*, January 23, 1874.
57. *San Joaquin Republican*, February 22, 1871.

CHAPTER II

FROM LOS ANGELES TO SAN FRANCISCO BY WAY OF FORT TEJON, VISALIA, GILROY, AND SAN JOSE 1855-1861

"The cry of 'Overland Stage' awakened me from pleasant dreams, and summoned me, reluctant, from a glorious feather bed."
—Mariposa Gazette, July 1, 1859

LOS ANGELES was some three hundred miles from the nearest gold rush mines and the town did not experience the degree of economic boom that occurred at Stockton in the early 1850s. Yet the town's merchants benefited from trade with the gold seekers who arrived by way of the southern trails, and the nearby ranchers drove beef cattle to markets in the mines. Extending northward from Los Angeles was a primitive road, El Camino Viejo. Scarcely were the gold seekers who followed it underway when they reached the precipitous San Fernando Mountains. Then the road turned northeast up San Francisquito Canyon to Elizabeth Lake, beyond which it crossed the Mojave Plains to the Tehachapi Mountains. Yet unlike the earlier travelers on El Camino Viejo, who went over these mountains by way of San Emigdio Pass to the west side of the San Joaquin Valley, the gold seekers went to the east side by way of Tejon Pass.[1] However, by the mid-1850s most traffic was crossing the Tehachapi Mountains by way of the so-called "New" Tejon Pass, located between San Emigdio and Tejon passes.[2] In the San Joaquin Valley the gold seekers followed the

Los Angeles and Stockton Road, which skirted the foothills of the Sierra Nevada east of the swampy lowlands. Along its northbound course were river crossings at Gordon's Ferry on the Kern, Poole's Ferry (and subsequently Smith's Ferry) on the Kings, Converse's Ferry on the San Joaquin, and Phillips' Ferry on the Merced.[3]

In the early 1850s the Indians living between the Tuolumne and Kaweah rivers became hostile to the miners who were overrunning their hunting grounds. Federal jurisdiction was established over the tribes after militia forces quelled an uprising. In September, 1853, an Indian reservation was created in Tejon Canyon, and construction was begun on Fort Tejon in Grapevine Canyon in August, 1854.[4] If Los Angeles businessmen opened a passable road over the San Fernando Mountains, the *Los Angeles Star* predicted that most of the supplies for these federal establishments would be purchased in Los Angeles.[5]

Among the Los Angeles businessmen who participated in road building in the San Fernando Mountains were David W. Alexander and Phineas Banning, whose ubiquitous stage and freight firm had its origins on the road between San Pedro and Los Angeles. When late in 1854 it became apparent that some sponsors were slow in contributing money, Banning boldly demonstrated the feasibility of the nearly completed project by driving a Concord stage over the mountains. But he barely escaped disaster as the swaying vehicle rolled down the steep north side. Nevertheless, Banning's feat facilitated the fund collecting, although the road work only slightly eased the climb over the mountains.[6] In January, 1855, Alexander and Banning advertised the beginning of stage and freight service between San Pedro and the Indian reservation by way of Los Angeles, San Fernando, Elizabeth Lake and Fort Tejon.[7]

Early in 1855 California underwent a financial crisis which ended the gold rush prosperity and widespread

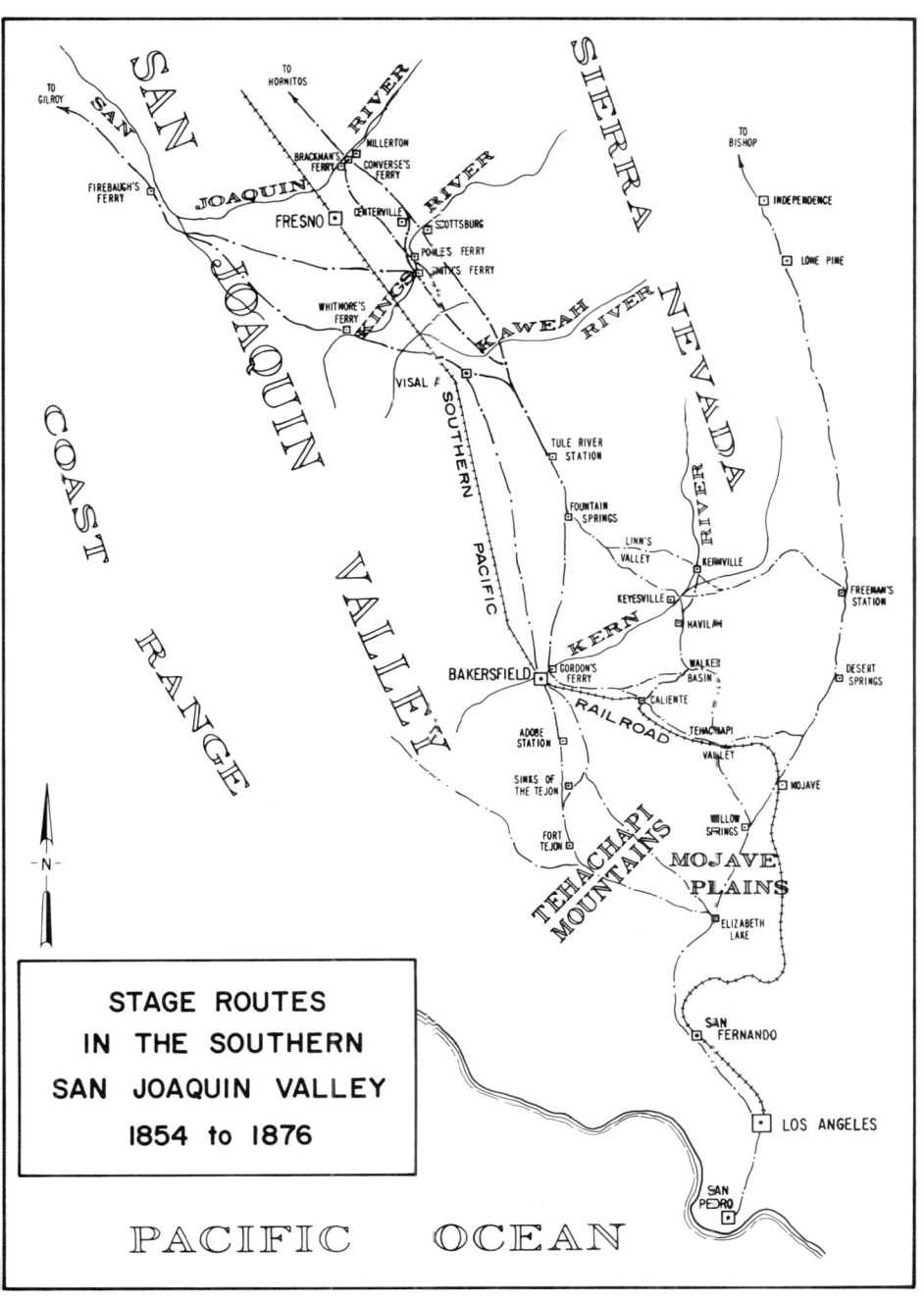

excitement over reportedly rich gold mines on the isolated Kern River. During a short-lived rush some five thousand gold seekers went to the supposed bonanzas in the southern Sierra Nevada. Although Alexander and Banning advertised that their stages went to the "Kern River gold mines,"[8] this claim was misleading, for the mines were in a mountainous area many miles northeast of the Indian reservation. A sojourner who knew that the stage passengers were deposited far short of the diggings recommended that the miners buy horses at Los Angeles and ride to the mines.[9] Alexander and Banning dissolved their partnership in the late 1850s when the former turned to cattle raising in the Tehachapi Mountains.[10] In May, 1858, the *San Francisco Alta California* described Banning as "a most indefatigable man" with stages and freight wagons "on all the highways, from San Pedro to the Colorado and the Tejon."[11]

The isolated Kern River mines were afforded stage service in the early 1860s by way of a connection with Visalia. In the meantime mail riders traveled between Los Angeles and Visalia by way of Keyesville, a mining town near the confluence of the North and South forks of the Kern River. When rider David Smith died in June, 1857, he was praised for his punctuality and disposition to accommodate.[12] Another rider, Charles Wilson, who was reported missing in April, 1858, presumably was killed by hostile Indians while delivering a $3,000 gold consignment to Los Angeles.[13]

Some New Yorkers, among whom was John Butterfield, organized the Overland Mail Company, and in September, 1857, their firm was granted a federal subsidy in support of passenger and mail service between Saint Louis and Memphis in the Mississippi Valley and San Francisco. The proprietors began preparations for staging over a so-called "oxbow route," that is, a southern one by way of Fort Smith, El Paso and Los Angeles. A year later the stage service was inaugurated from an

Phineas Banning. (Courtesy, California State Library)

eastern railhead at Tipton, Missouri.[14] In the meantime the stocking of the Overland Mail Company's way stations between Tucson and San Francisco had been accomplished by division superintendent Marcus L. Kinyon. In doing this, Kinyon pointed out the need for further road work in the rugged San Fernando Mountains. An improvement project was undertaken jointly by the Los Angeles businessmen and the County of Los Angeles.[15]

The Overland Mail Company, ahead of full operations between Tipton and San Francisco, in August, 1858, placed stages on the road between Los Angeles and San Francisco.[16] A month later, in September, full service was inaugurated. "Think of that!" asserted the *San Francisco Alta California* when the first eastbound stage left for Tipton. In October the newspaper announced the arrival of the first westbound stage, with the horses running "at a tearing gallop."[17] A correspondent of the *New York Herald* was the only through westbound passenger, and he was especially impressed with the impromptu celebration which greeted the stage upon its arrival at Visalia. Although the town was reached near midnight, a group of well-wishers gathered and celebrated the event with a loud anvil salute. The celebrants cheered loudly as the stage left for San Francisco.[18]

From Los Angeles the Overland Mail Company's stages reached Fort Tejon by way of the road taken earlier by those of David W. Alexander and Phineas Banning. Beyond a descent of Grapevine Canyon to the San Joaquin Valley the road turned northeast by way of the Sinks of the Tejon to Gordon's Ferry on the Kern River. Upon leaving the foothills north of the river, it crossed the plains to Visalia, which was in the verdant Four Creeks country. Turning northwest from Visalia, the road went to Whitmore's Ferry on the Kings River and Firebaugh's Ferry on the San Joaquin River. From the latter river the road ran to Pacheco pass in the Diablo

Range, which it crossed to Gilroy. From there the road went northwest through San Jose to San Francisco.[19] At first Concord stages were used only between San Francisco and San Jose, while canvas-covered thoroughbrace wagons carried the passengers between San Jose and Los Angeles. However, in May, 1860, Concord stages were placed on the road between San Jose and Visalia.[20]

At isolated Visalia the arrival of the Overland Mail Company's stages with the latest news, according to the *Tulare County Record* in September, 1859, was anticipated "with almost as much anxiety" as that of the steamers at the coastal towns.[21] In that month Horace Greeley, a well-known Republican journalist, reportedly was a passenger on a stage scheduled to arrive at midnight. Visalia's "best citizens" planned a reception for him, and they aroused friends "from their slumbers," including the only Republican in town. When the embarrassed Republican realized that the "distinguished" visitor was only a company agent, he left "amid the shouts of the assembled multitude."[22]

In July, 1860, the *Visalia Delta* reported that "new mining discoveries" east of the Sierra Nevada were "creating ... an excitement" in many parts of California. The stages arriving at Visalia were "loaded to overflowing" with passengers, many of whom were enroute to the trans-Sierran mining districts.[23] Mostly their destinations were between the Coso Range in the south and Mono Lake in the north, including the intervening Owens Valley.

The Overland Mail Company's stages had been arriving ahead of schedule at Visalia for some time when in October, 1859, there was a delay. Anxious Visalians awaited the news of "some terrible disaster," but later they found that a storm had detained the stage near the Colorado River.[24] In December, 1860, a northbound stage was slowed by snowfall between Los Angeles and Fort Tejon. Another stage en route from San Francisco to

Visalia during a rainstorm fell twelve hours behind schedule.[25] During heavy rains which caused streams to overflow their banks, a stage was on the road between Visalia and Fort Tejon for three days in January, 1861.[26]

In the meantime some of the Overland Mail Company's drivers had been involved in accidents between Los Angeles and Visalia. In March, 1860, for example, Victor Kinson was driving between Fort Tejon and Visalia when a bridle broke. In jumping from his seat "to secure the horse," Kinson fractured a leg.[27] In that same month Jacob W. Brickerhoff's stage upset in a slough south of Visalia. Although no passengers were hurt, the driver's legs were broken.[28] When Aseal W. Winslow was driving south from Fort Tejon in September, 1860, a "gale of wind" upset the stage and it fell on him, rendering him "speechless for several hours." One passenger was somewhat injured, but the others received only slight bruises.[29]

In a May, 1860, leadership change, John Butterfield, heretofore president of the Overland Mail Company, was succeeded by William B. Dinsmore.[30] During the latter's presidency Indians in the Southwest became troublesome, and the Civil War made it difficult to operate within the Confederacy. Therefore, the Overland Mail Company was authorized to transfer its operations to a central route, and in April, 1861, the company ceased to operate in the San Joaquin Valley.[31] While on their way to Salt Lake City in May, Overland Mail Company employees from Arizona reached Visalia with 150 horses and seventeen wagons. In July other employees from Texas passed through the town with sixty horses and mules, together with seven Concord coaches.[32] From Los Angeles came a report that the withdrawal of the Overland Mail Company from the southern route was having "a disastrous effect upon business." Besides the ending of overland stage travel between Los Angeles and the Mississippi Valley, the town lost an important communicative link with the San Joaquin Valley.[33]

Notes

1. Frank F. Latta, *El Camino Viejo a Los Angeles*, 4.
2. Helen S. Giffin and Arthur Woodward, *The Story of El Tejon*, 13.
3. Wallace Smith, *Garden of the Sun*, 152-53.
4. Giffin and Woodward, op. cit., 21, 59.
5. *Los Angeles Star*, June 24, 1854.
6. Horace Bell, *Reminiscences of a Ranger*, 335-37.
7. *San Francisco Alta California*, January 23, 1855.
8. *Ibid.*
9. *Ibid.*, February 25, 1855.
10. Alexander and Banning's original partnership was dissolved in the late 1850s, but they formed a new one in the mid-1860s. Mayme Krythe, *Port Admiral: Phineas Banning, 1830-1885*, 82, 133; William H. Brewer, *Up and Down California in 1860-1864*, 385-86.
11. *San Francisco Alta California*, May 29, 1858.
12. Benjamin I. Hayes, *Scrapbooks*, no. 68, in the Bancroft Library.
13. *San Francisco Alta California*, April 29, 1858.
14. Roscoe P. Conkling and Margaret B. Conkling, *The Butterfield Overland Mail, 1857-1869*, I, 124.
15. Vernette S. Ripley, "The San Fernando Pass and the Pioneer Traffic that Went over It," *Historical Society of Southern California Quarterly*, XXX, no. 1 (March, 1948), 44-45.
16. *Ibid.*, 45-46.
17. *San Francisco Alta California*, September 15, October 11, 1858.
18. Waterman L. Ormsby, *The Butterfield Overland Mail*, 119-20.
19. *Ibid.*, 114-30.
20. *Visalia Delta*, May 12, 1860.
21. *Tulare County Record*, September 3, 17, 1859.
22. *Ibid.*, September 10, 1859.
23. *Visalia Delta*, July 7, 1860.
24. *Tulare County Record*, October 1, 1859.
25. *Visalia Delta*, December 22, 29, 1860.
26. *Ibid.*, January 12, 1861.

27. *Ibid.*, March 10, 1860.
28. *Ibid.*, March 31, 1860.
29. *Ibid.*, September 15, 1860.
30. *Ibid.*, May 12, 1860.
31. *Ibid.*, April 13, 20, 1861.
32. *Ibid.*, May 30, July 11, 1861.
33. *San Francisco Alta California*, April 27, 1861.

CHAPTER III

From Visalia to Hornitos
by way of Scottsburg
and Millerton
1857-1872

*"Variety of scenery, a good natural road, good
teams, and a driver you can trust, are...
agreeable accompaniments of travel."*
—*Visalia Delta*, December 22, 1860

WHILE THE short-lived Kern River gold rush was underway in the spring of 1855, several thousand gold seekers made the long trip to the remote southern Sierra Nevada. There they were beyond the reach of regular mail and express communication. During the gold excitement some hastily enlisted northbound express riders left Keyesville, a mining town on the river, but none returned to the mines. A correspondent of the *San Joaquin Republican* suggested that this refuted the old adage that "whatever goes up must come down." The Kern River rush had run its course and only a few hundred gold seekers were on the river by June when Thomas M. Heston provided a "rabbit skin" express service that linked Keyesville, Visalia and Mariposa.[1]

In September, 1857, by which time Heston had settled in Visalia, he advertised in the *San Joaquin Republican* his purchase of "a four horse coach and splendid team" and arrangements for passenger comfort along the some one hundred and fifty miles between Visalia and Hornitos. In addition the stages carried mail and express shipments. From Visalia the stages went north along the

Los Angeles and Stockton Road by way of Scottsburg on the Kings River and Millerton on the San Joaquin River.[2] At Hornitos Heston's stages connected with A. N. Fisher and Company for trips to Stockton and Mariposa. Subsequently his stages connected at Visalia with the Overland Mail Company when in September, 1858, the latter began to operate between the Mississippi Valley and San Francisco.

Although Heston continued to operate his express business between Visalia and Hornitos, he sold the stage line in June, 1859, to an employee, William L. Hice, of Millerton.[3] In July the editor of the *Tulare County Record* reported that Hice's stage line was doing a good business.[4] In the following month Amos O. Thoms, a Visalia hotelkeeper, became an agent for the stage company. The acquisition of some good four-horse teams helped lessen the travel time, and the accommodations assertedly surpassed those of any "similar conveyance in the state." According to the *Visalia Delta*, the speed achieved on Hice's stage line equalled, if not surpassed, that of the Overland Mail Company.[5]

In mid-1859 a decade of desultory mining activity east of the Sierra Nevada ended with the discovery of rich mineral deposits in the Washoe Valley. Within a year wide-ranging prospectors had reached Mono Lake, the Owens Valley and the Coso Range. A rush of wealth seekers to the trans-Sierran mining districts was underway in July, 1860, when the *Visalia Delta* reported that heavily-loaded stages were arriving at Visalia. The hotel accommodations were insufficient to take care of the "transient population."[6] The Overland Mail Company's stages from San Francisco were "constantly crowded," but those of Hice and Wilson were "running light." For this reason the *Visalia Delta* reminded travelers that, besides the stage route over Pacheco Pass, there was another by steamer and stage through Stockton.[7] In December Amos O. Thoms ended his role as an agent for

Millerton on the San Joaquin River in 1873. (Courtesy, California State Library)

Hice and Company, and William L. Hice formed a partnership with John Wilson, a well-known stage agent for A. N. Fisher and Company at Stockton.[8]

With the beginning of the Civil War in April, 1861, the Overland Mail Company ceased to operate by way of Visalia, and Hice and Wilson afforded the only stage connection with the outside world. The proprietors were compensated for the increased amount of mail they handled by a more lucrative contract.[9] In contrast to the proclaimed pro-South sympathies of many Visalians, Hice and Wilson's stage driver reached the town on the Fourth of July patriotically flying the Stars and Stripes over each horse.[10]

Widespread rainstorms drenched the San Joaquin Valley in January, 1862, and the Los Angeles and Stockton Road between Visalia and Hornitos became so muddy and rutted that it was virtually impassable for stages. Hice and Wilson's stable at Millerton was washed away, and the horses were turned "out to grass." It was uncertain when stage service would be resumed.[11] The editor of the *Visalia Delta* was desperate for exchange newspapers when William L. Hice and a driver, Aseal W. Winslow, arrived with the "letter mail" and a copy of the *San Francisco Alta California*.[12] Since the stages were not running by April, the editor feared that the miners who otherwise would go to the trans-Sierran mines by way of Visalia were going instead by steamer to Los Angeles. As a result Visalians were losing "much money."[13] Because Hice and Wilson's stage company was not making the required mail deliveries by April, the proprietors lost the mail contract.[14]

Hice and Wilson's stage company was out of business in May, 1862, at a time of increasing travel, and A. N. Fisher and Company began to run stages between Visalia and Hornitos.[15] Moreover, in July Amos O. Thoms, who earlier had been an agent for William L. Hice, began to operate a "mail line of stages." The *Visalia Delta* reported that his good teams and new coaches were handled by "careful, experienced, and accommodating drivers."[16] When in December A. N. Fisher and Company ceased to operate to Visalia, the proprietors advertised instead a connection with Thoms' stage line at Hornitos.[17]

Although Amos O. Thoms owned the stage firm that operated between Visalia and Hornitos until the mid-1860s, he became more involved in the management of the Telegraph Stage Company, which he organized in June, 1863, to connect Visalia and Gilroy. He ceased to advertise the schedule of his older company in the *Visalia Delta* in July, 1864. By June, 1866, if not earlier, Israel W. Davis had acquired the mail-carrying stage line that operated between Visalia and Hornitos.[18]

The mining activity around Millerton had declined so decidedly by December, 1865, that a resident characterized the town as "much at one side of the rest of creation." The stages continued to go by way of the "nearly forgotten" settlement, but through travelers crossed the San Joaquin River two miles downstream at Brackman's Ferry.[19] During almost incessant rains which began to fall in December, 1866, and continued into January, Millerton was partly destroyed by the rampaging San Joaquin River. High water in the Kings River wrecked Smith's Ferry, as well as washed away Scottsburg. For a month only small amounts of mail reached Visalia, but finally a "half stage load of mail matter" was delivered late in January by way of Hornitos. In February regular stage runs were resumed between Visalia and Hornitos.[20] In August, 1866, Centerville, located on higher ground west of Scottsburg, had been described as "a little off the line of travel." Yet after the destruction of ill-fated Scottsburg, Israel W. Davis advertised in June, 1867, that his stages were going by way of Centerville.[21]

In May, 1868, the *Visalia Delta* reported that the stage company operating between Visalia and Hornitos had been sold to Patrick Bennett, who lived at Union, a stage station located twenty miles south of Hornitos on Mariposa Creek.[22] Bennett's stages had been carrying the mail for about two years when in July, 1870, the *Fresno Expositor* expressed outrage over the awarding of the contract to speculating out-of-staters. After Bennett refused to carry the mail on their terms, presumably the postal authorities enabled the contractors to escape liability by abandoning the route.[23] When the mail deliveries by way of Hornitos ceased, the unhappy residents of Millerton and Visalia petitioned for a restoration of the service.[24]

After being awarded a contract to carry the mail between Stockton and Visalia, Lemuel H. Silman in July sent stages by way of Tuolumne City and Paradise City on the Tuolumne River to Snelling, where they turned south through Millerton to Visalia.[25] Millerton residents preferred Bennett's accommodating service, and they characterized that of Silman as "an outrageous humbug."[26] It was rumored in October that Silman was endeavoring to acquire Bennett's stage line, but instead Silman withdrew his stages in November. Following the awarding of a mail contract to Bennett, the *Fresno Expositor* reported that the residents of Millerton were "feeling both thankful and happy."[27]

While S. and Z. Fisher's Stage Line was operating from the San Joaquin Valley Railroad at Modesto in April, 1871, Patrick Bennett arranged a connection with the stage firm's Mariposa line at Snelling. Inasmuch as the new arrangement shortened the travel time to San Francisco, the *Fresno Expositor* described it as "a most acceptable change."[28] While Bennett's "stock and stages were good," according to a traveler, the distances between stopping places were "long and tedious."[29] In December stations for changing horses were established at Sheep Camp between Visalia and the Kings River and at Red Banks between the Kings River and Millerton.[30]

Notwithstanding the skill and care of the stage drivers

on the trips between Visalia and Hornitos, bad weather and poor road conditions contributed to occasional accidents. Thomas M. Heston owned the stage line when in March, 1859, a driver attempted to ford swollen Mariposa Creek. The vehicle overturned and was swept downstream, but all aboard were able to escape. Yet the mail and express were lost, and the horses drowned.[31] During William L. Hice's proprietorship in June, 1860, a stage upset soon after the driver left Hornitos. Two passengers were severely injured. Another upset occurred in that same area in December, but there was no material damage.[32] During a rainstorm in December, 1871, Patrick Bennett and a driver, Russell H. Fleming, nearly lost their lives in the raging Chowchilla River. When the stage became mired in quicksand, they freed the horses, but one of them drowned. Rescuers helped pull the stage from the torrent, it was refitted with horses, and the trip was resumed.[33]

Southbound construction on the San Joaquin Valley Railroad reached Merced in January, 1872, and both Patrick Bennett and the Telegraph Stage Company routed their stages to a railhead connection in the following month. On the trip between Visalia and Merced, Bennett's stages crossed the San Joaquin River at Jones' Ferry, while those of the Telegraph Stage Company crossed downstream at Firebaugh's Ferry.[34] When the San Joaquin Valley Railroad reached Fresno in May, 1872, Bennett limited his stage service to runs northeast to Millerton and southeast to Centerville.[35]

NOTES

1. *San Joaquin Republican*, June 16, 1855.
2. *Ibid.*, September 27, 1857.
3. *Mariposa Gazette*, June 17, 1859.
4. *Tulare County Record*, July 2, 1859.
5. *Visalia Delta*, October 22, November 5, 1859.
6. *Ibid.*, July 7, 1860.
7. *Ibid.*, September 1, 1860.
8. *Ibid.*, December 8, 1860.
9. *Ibid.*, April 13, 1861.
10. *Ibid.*, July 11, 1861.
11. *San Joaquin Republican*, February 1, 1862.
12. *Visalia Delta*, February 13, 1862. The stage driver popularly known as "Long Tom" was Aseal W. Winslow.
13. *Ibid.*, April 17, 1862.
14. *Ibid.*, April 10, 1862.
15. *Ibid.*, May 22, 1862.
16. *Ibid.*, July 3, 1862.
17. *Stockton Independent*, December 2, 1862.
18. *Visalia Delta*, April 11, 1866; Sonora's *American Flag*, quoted in the *Mariposa Gazette*, June 30, 1866. S. and Z. Fisher's Stage Line continued to advertise in the *Stockton Independent* that its stages connected with those of "A. O. Thomas" until February 12, 1867, when his name was replaced with that of "I. W. Davis." It was not unusual for the stage companies to let their advertisements become out-of-date.
19. *Visalia Delta*, December 6, 1865; Wallace Smith, *Garden of the Sun*, 152.
20. *Visalia Delta*, January 29, February 5, March 4, 1868.
21. *Ibid.*, August 22, 1866, June 12, 1867.
22. *Ibid.*, May 13, 1868; John Outcalt, *History of Merced County, California*, 111.
23. *Fresno Expositor*, July 20, 1870.
24. *Ibid.*, July 27, 1870; *Visalia Delta*, July 27, 1870.
25. *San Joaquin Valley Argus*, July 9, 1870; *Visalia Delta*, August 3, 1870.
26. *Fresno Expositor*, November 30, 1870.
27. *Ibid.*, December 14, 1870.
28. *Ibid.*, March 29, 1871.

29. *Visalia Delta*, August 10, 1871.
30. *Ibid.*, December 28, 1871.
31. *Mariposa Gazette*, March 25, 1859.
32. *Visalia Delta*, June 30, December 8, 1860.
33. *Ibid.*, January 4, 1872.
34. *Fresno Expositor*, February 7, 1872.
35. *Visalia Delta*, May 9, 1872.

Amos O. Thoms. (Courtesy, Tulare County Museum)

CHAPTER IV

From Visalia to San Jose by way of Whitmore's and Firebaugh's Ferries, and Gilroy
1863-1872

"Thoms' stage ... carried away ten passengers, whose aggregate weight was about 1,900 pounds—four ... weighing a little over nine hundred pounds."
—*Visalia Delta*, March 17, 1869

In July, 1860, the businessmen of Visalia were prospering, according to the *Visalia Delta*, for the town was full of strangers, many of whom were going to newly discovered mines in the Owens Valley. The farming activity was increasing in the countryside, where already established settlers were being joined by newcomers.[1] Yet within a year the general optimism began to wane, and for good reason. In April, 1861, the Overland Mail Company ceased to operate by way of Visalia. Then the Owens Valley Indians became hostile, and this slowed the flow of miners and merchandise eastward over the Sierra Nevada. Unusually heavy rains in January, 1862, worsened conditions by causing widespread destruction in the San Joaquin Valley. Following the rains the *Visalia Delta* urged the businessmen to do all they could to hasten economic recovery. The farmers, rather than "fold their arms and curse the flood," were encouraged to produce abundant crops.[2]

By the spring of 1863 most of the Owens Valley Indians were peaceful, and gold seekers again were migrating to the trans-Sierran districts. Two years after the Overland Mail Company had withdrawn, Amos O. Thoms, a Visalia hotelkeeper, organized the Telegraph Stage Company in June, 1863, and restored service between Visalia and Gilroy.[3] From the latter town the Coast Line Stage Company afforded a connection with San Francisco by way of San Jose. In July the *Visalia Delta* reported that the Telegraph Stage Company was well patronized. Moreover, Union sympathizers who went by way of Gilroy avoided "those pestiferous secession holes, Millerton and Snelling."[4]

When construction on the San Francisco and San Jose Railroad reached Redwood City in October, 1863, a railhead connection was arranged by the Telegraph Stage Company.[5] Yet by the time the railroad was completed in January, 1864, the stages had retreated to San Jose.[6] The appreciative *Visalia Delta* asserted that Thoms' stages made Visalia a virtual "suburb of San Francisco." Visalians visited the coastal city to hear lectures, attend theaters and fish in San Francisco Bay.[7]

During the first year of its operation the Telegraph Stage Company was not afforded the economic benefit of a mail contract, and one awarded to Thoms in July, 1864, was not reawarded a year later. Yet, as the *Visalia Delta* explained, his stages continued to carry the mail as a "personal responsibility."[8] Upon being assured of a mail contract in July, 1866, Thoms purchased "dashing and flashing" stagecoaches, which added a "finishing touch to his enterprise."[9] Through the acquisition of an already-operating stage line in October, 1867, the Telegraph Stage Company was expanded southeast from Visalia to Havilah in the Kern River mines by way of Linn's Valley and Kernville. Characterizing Thoms as "a real live man and deserving of success," the *Visalia Delta* asserted that the passengers were afforded all the expected comforts on the long trip between San Jose and Havilah.[10]

Visalia businesses in about 1864. [Courtesy, Annie Mitchell]

When the Telegraph Stage Company began to operate in June, 1863, the San Joaquin Valley was in the throes of a prolonged drought. Yet as unpleasant as was travel over the dusty roads, with the coming of heavy rains in February, 1866, it became difficult, and sometimes impossible, to travel over the muddy roads. Nonetheless the *Visalia Delta* reported that the drivers only failed to "come to time" on a few trips during the worst weather. Considerable hardship was experienced in the hauling of supplies to the stage stations.[11]

When a year later in January, 1867, heavy rains delayed the stages for several days, the lack of mail deliveries caused what the *Visalia Delta* described as "an elongation of the public countenance." The residents "surmised all imaginable reasons for the delay." When a small amount of mail finally reached Visalia, there was "not a letter for husband, lover, or businessman," and the newspapers were "a mass of thoroughly prepared pulp." The stage had overturned in swollen Pacheco Creek, and most of the water-soaked mail was left to dry at Firebaugh's Ferry.[12]

Almost incessant rains which began to fall in the San Joaquin Valley in December, 1867, continued well into January, and the resulting high water in Fresno Slough disrupted travel between Whitmore's and Firebaugh's ferries. Since Thoms could not get vehicles over the road, the *Visalia Delta* was sure that is was "useless for anyone else to try."[13] The storm was over when in February he spent ten days preparing for the resumption of operations. Yet until the water in Fresno Slough receded in August, Thoms' drivers, instead of crossing the Kings River at Whitmore's Ferry, went northward from Visalia to a crossing at Smith's Ferry, beyond which they turned west toward Firebaugh's Ferry.[14]

For several months after the rains had ended the stage drivers experienced difficulties on a newly-built stretch of road between Cross Creek and Smith's Ferry. While a

Henry M. Newhall. (Courtesy, Bancroft Library)

driver was passing a stalled wagon in April, 1868, the stage upset, and the mail, baggage and passengers were soaked. When two weeks later a stage upset, some mail, express and baggage were lost in the water. The passengers swam to safety. A driver's horses became bogged in mud in May, and he unhitched them, only to have them run to the Kings River. The stranded passengers spent the night without food or lodging. A few days later a stage dropped into a mudhole, and driver Solomon S. Lefurgey was thrown onto the running gear. Fortunately he retained control over the horses.[15] Until August, wagons, rather than stages, were driven over the rough road between Visalia and Firebaugh's Ferry. Anyone but Thoms, it was asserted, would have abandoned the stage line under such adverse weather conditions, and he was praised for having maintained "communication with the outside world."[16]

Less severe rainy seasons during 1869 and 1870 afforded the Telegraph Stage Company's drivers a respite from the difficulties they had experienced during the preceding three winters. Yet in December, 1871, prolonged rains again disrupted travel, especially between Firebaugh's Ferry and Gilroy. A passenger who was aboard a stage that left Visalia in a rainstorm described the hazardous trip for the *Inyo Independent*. The trip went "tolerably well" as far as Firebaugh's Ferry, but on the plains to the northwest the horses occasionally were "all in a pile; all down in the mud at once." In Pacheco Pass there were several hazardous fordings of Pacheco Creek, and at one of these the stage drifted 600 feet. A flood had destroyed a bridge in the Santa Clara Valley, and the passengers were taken by boat and wagon over the last two and a half miles to Gilroy.[17]

In the meantime southward construction on the Santa Clara and Pajaro Valley Railroad had forced the Telegraph Stage Company to retreat from San Jose to Gilroy by March, 1869.[18] Two years later, in April, 1871, Thoms sold the stage company to a group of San Francisco businessmen, the best known of whom was Henry M. Newhall. He had been active in the building of the San Francisco and San Jose and the Santa Clara and Pajaro Valley railroads. At first the advertised proprietors were William G. Roberts and Daniel George, who were stage agents in San Francisco, but in September, 1872, their names were supplanted by that of Newhall.[19] In the meantime, in June, 1871, the company advertised that the line had been "restocked with the best quality of new coaches."[20]

When southbound construction on the San Joaquin Valley Railroad reached Merced in February, 1872, the Telegraph Stage Company ceased to operate from Gilroy.[21] Starting with a railhead connection at Merced, the stage drivers retreated before the advancing railroad until they were operating from Fresno in May and Goshen in August.[22] In May, 1872, Amos O. Thoms, the firm's former owner, became its general manager.[23] Beyond Goshen the railroad company claimed a land grant, and it was known as the Southern Pacific. Since the railroad passed no closer than six miles to Visalia, a newspaperman regretted that the citizens of the by-passed town had not thought of "building all their houses on wheels."[24]

NOTES

1. *Visalia Delta*, July 14, 1860.
2. *Ibid.*, January 30, 1862.
3. *Ibid.*, June 4, 11, 18, 1863.
4. *Ibid.*, July 23, 1863.
5. *Ibid.*, October 15, 1863.
6. *Ibid.*, January 21, 1864.
7. *Ibid.*, June 14, 1865.
8. *Ibid.*, June 23, 1864, April 11, 1866.
9. *Ibid.*, May 9, 1866.
10. *Ibid.*, December 4, 1867. Apparently no file of the *Havilah Courier* for October, 1867, exists, but the company's advertisement on January 4, 1868, indicated that it was

changed on November 2, 1867, in order to show a change in ownership of the company.
11. *Visalia Delta*, February 14, 1866.
12. *Ibid.*, January 30, 1867.
13. *Ibid.*, January 22, 29, 1868.
14. *Ibid.*, January 22, February 12, August 26, 1868.
15. *Ibid.*, April 15, 29, May 6, 20, 1868.
16. *Ibid.*, August 26, 1868.
17. *Inyo Independent*, January 6, 1872.
18. *Visalia Delta*, March 10, 17, 1869.
19. Amos O. Thoms' sale of the Telegraph Stage Company was reported by the *Inyo Independent*, April 15, 1871, and on November 16, 1871, the *Visalia Delta* reported that "sometime ago" the company had "passed into the hands of H. M. Newhall of San Francisco." The company's advertisement in the *Visalia Delta*, June 1, 1871, did not list a proprietor, but one in the *Inyo Independent*, August 19, 1871, listed Roberts and George as the proprietors. Their names were replaced by that of Newhall in the *Inyo Independent*, September 28, 1872.
20. *Visalia Delta*, June 1, 1871.
21. *Ibid.*, February 1, 1872.
22. *Ibid.*, May 9, 1872.
23. *Ibid.*
24. *Ibid.*, June 6, 1872.

CHAPTER V

FROM VISALIA TO THE KERN RIVER MINES AND LONE PINE, AND FROM LOS ANGELES 1862-1872

"A trip to Clear Creek, which formerly was looked upon with dread, ... is now a ... real pleasure trip."
—Visalia Delta, March 14, 1866

IN MARCH, 1860, the *Visalia Delta* reported that "the regular periodical stampede for supposed new and rich mines" was underway. The springtime destinations of many who contracted the "peregrinating contagion" were in the mines east of the Sierra Nevada. "Symptoms of the Mono Lake mania" were apparent among the restless Kern River miners who departed for the developing mineral district. Soon they were joined by Visalians who hoped to find wealth east of the Sierra Nevada.[1] By July the news from the Coso Range was setting San Franciscans "agog to know ... more of the new rival of Washoe." By then even the "outside chances" were being engaged on the stages destined for Visalia.[2] Aware that the businessmen in the northern counties were attempting to control the mining trade, the *Visalia Delta* urged the local merchants to "awaken from their lethargy" and seek a share of the trade with the mining camps east of the Sierra Nevada.[3]

Although only primitive roads in the Sierra Nevada led to Walker Pass, several teamsters left Visalia with merchandise in April, 1860. Some drove their wagons south along the Los Angeles and Stockton Road to Caliente Creek and climbed to the Los Angeles and Keyesville Road, reaching the upper Kern River by way of Walker Basin. Others climbed from Fountain Springs to Linn's Valley, where they began a difficult ascent and descent of the Greenhorn Mountains. From the Kern River mines the teamsters drove east up the South Fork Valley to Walker Pass.[4] The difficulties they experienced in the Greenhorn Mountains dramatized the need for road work over this rugged spur of the Sierra Nevada. The *Visalia Delta* reported in March, 1861, that work was underway in the mountains, but much of this was destroyed by the heavy rains in January, 1862.[5]

In April, 1861, John Wilson, one of the proprietors of Hice and Wilson's stage line, which connected Visalia and Hornitos, joined John A. Young, an express rider, in extending stage service from Visalia to Linn's Valley.[6] Within less than a year the devastating rains of January, 1862, temporarily halted stage operations. Among those who restored the stage lines was Thomas M. Heston, who five years earlier had inaugurated service between Visalia and Hornitos. By July, 1862, his mail-carrying stages were operating between Visalia and Keyesville by way of Linn's Valley.[7] When winter was at hand in December, the stages were withdrawn, and the mail was carried on horseback. Yet Heston announced that in the spring he intended "to run a line of stages through to Slate Range."[8] While returning from a business trip to the trans-Sierran mines in June, 1863, he failed to reach Visalia. Heston's fate was unknown until August, 1864, when his remains were discovered at the site of a presumed ambush near Nine Mile Canyon north of Walker Pass.[9]

Although the Owens Valley Indians might have tolerated mining activities in the surrounding mountains, they grew restive when white men began to occupy the "grassy patches" where the natives gathered food. Their hostilities brought mining and ranching to a virtual standstill. After leading an expedition of Second Cavalry, California Volunteers, to the Owens Valley, Lieutenant-Colonel George S. Evans established Camp Independence in July, 1862.[10] Within a year the Indians were fairly peaceful, and in August, 1863, the *Visalia Delta* reported that miners and ranchers in a steady stream were reaching the Owens Valley.[11]

In June, 1863, the Owens Valley Stage Line, which was organized by Visalians James C. White, Charles Rice and Charles H. Schleigh, began to operate between Visalia and Camp Independence by way of Linn's Valley and Keyesville. According to a newspaper correspondent, the firm handled "the mail and express when it scarcely paid expenses, in all kinds of weather, and in times of danger." The mail generated by Camp Independence afforded a large portion of the receipts, and consequently the proprietors suffered a serious setback when the "post mail" was discontinued in September. James C. White was "a Union man," and presumably the postal inspector was "stubbornly indifferent" to anyone who favored the Union.[12]

By the mid-1860s the Kern River mines were attracting renewed interest, and the most promising of these were near Kernville along the North Fork of the Kern River and around Havilah between Keyesville and Walker Basin. Upon the completion of the carefully surveyed McFarlane Road eastward over the Greenhorn Mountains in March, 1864, Charles Rice and Freeman S. Raymond, whose stages already were running between Visalia and Linn's Valley, extended their line to Kernville. At the latter town the proprietors made available saddle animals for the use of individuals destined for the Owens Valley.[13]

Havilah's mines were booming when the *Visalia Delta* commended Hiram Meade and Israel W. Davis for their "energy in the management" of a new stage line.[14] Scarcely had they started runs between Visalia and the new mining town than in April, 1865, a Havilah-bound stage was "heavily draped... in mourning" for assassinated President Abraham Lincoln.[15] In November Davis sold his interest in the line to William H. Clarke, a Visalia businessman, who in turn became the sole owner after he bought out Meade in July, 1867.[16] Amos O. Thoms acquired the stage line in November and annexed it to the Telegraph Stage Company, which was operating between Visalia and San Jose. He placed "first class stage wagons" on the road between Visalia and Havilah.[17] A patron reported that Thoms' drivers understood their business and made "any reasonable sacrifice for the safety and comfort" of the passengers. There were only moderate charges, it was reported, for accommodations that were generally good.[18]

In the meantime the *Los Angeles News* had urged the Los Angeles businessmen to support an effort to improve the northbound road leading to Havilah.[19] The project was completed by June, 1866, and the newspaper explained that San Franciscans could reach the mines in six days. Four of these were aboard a coastal steamer to Los Angeles and two were "easy travel" by stage to Havilah.[20] From Elizabeth Lake on the Los Angeles and Stockton Road the stages went north across the Mojave Plains to the Tehachapi Valley by way of Willow Springs and Oak Creek Pass. Leaving the valley by way of White Rock Creek, they crossed rugged mountains to Tollgate Canyon. Beyond Caliente Creek the stages went west to Walker Basin, where they turned north to Havilah, which was some one hundred and fifty miles from Los Angeles.[21]

While the road improvement work was underway, John J. Tomlinson, a well-known stage proprietor, placed "two new and elegant coaches" in service between Los Angeles and Havilah in June, 1865.[22] Since the coastal steamers sailed so irregularly between San Francisco and Los Angeles, most Havilah-bound travelers went by

Havilah, boom town of the 1860s. (Courtesy, Kern County Museum)

way of the San Joaquin Valley. Tomlinson withdrew his stages in October.[23] There were better prospects for profits when he resumed service in January, 1866, and he was awarded a mail contract in April, 1867.[24] After Tomlinson's death in June, 1867, Samuel Harper, Henry W. Robinson, John Collister and George W. Andrews, among others, owned the stage line until the early 1870s.

When the Owens Valley mines were booming in August, 1869, Amos O. Thoms extended the Telegraph Stage Company beyond Kernville to Lone Pine. Although the unprofitable line was abandoned in November, Thoms kept saddle horses at Kernville for the accommodation of travelers destined for the trans-Sierran mines.[25] The Telegraph Stage Company resumed its operations to Lone Pine in August, 1870, and the *Inyo Independent* was pleased that the Owens Valley again was "within five days of San Francisco."[26] Yet after Henry M. Newhall and other San Francisco businessmen acquired the Telegraph Stage Company and ceased to advertise its schedule in the *Inyo Independent*, the newspaper charged the mismanaged firm with operating "in the interest of second-rate hotels."[27]

In May, 1871, the *Inyo Independent* reported that Henry W. Robinson had established a stage line linking Los Angeles and Lone Pine. Calling this "a commendable enterprise," the newspaper urged the traveling public to afford his enterprise "the most substantial of support."[28] The proprietor, without the benefit of a mail contract, began to operate by way of Havilah and Walker Pass, which involved considerable mountain travel. When Robinson was authorized to carry the mail between Los Angeles and Lone Pine in February, 1872, he routed his stages more directly by way of Desert Springs east of the Sierra Nevada.[29] In March the *Inyo Independent* reported that his line was "well established, running on time, and doing a good business."[30] Yet Robinson withdrew his stages in August when the Telegraph Stage Company was selected to deliver the mail to Lone Pine by way of Havilah.[31] A month earlier that company had extended its operations southward from Visalia to Los Angeles by way of Bakersfield and Fort Tejon.

NOTES
1. *Visalia Delta*, March 3, 10, 17, 1860.
2. *San Francisco Alta California*, July 28, 1860.
3. *Visalia Delta*, March 31, 1860.
4. *Ibid.*, April 28, 1860.
5. *Ibid.*, March 9, 30, April 20, May 25, 1861, September 25, 1862.
6. *Ibid.*, April 27, 1861.
7. *Ibid.*, July 3, 1862.
8. *Ibid.*, December 25, 1862.
9. *Ibid.*, July 2, 1863, August 31, 1864.
10. United States, War Department, *The War of the Rebellion: A Compilation of the Official Records of the Union and Confederate Armies*, Series 1, Vol. 50, Pt. 1, 146-48.
11. *Visalia Delta*, August 27, 1863.
12. *Ibid.*, June 25, September 24, 1863.
13. *Ibid.*, March 17, 31, 1864.
14. *Ibid.*, October 4, 1865.
15. *Ibid.*, April 19, 1865.
16. *Ibid.*, November 15, 1865, July 10, 1867.
17. *Ibid.*, December 4, 1867. Apparently copies of the *Visalia Delta* and *Havilah Courier* for October and November are unavailable. The *Visalia Delta*, December 4, 1867, mentioned a change in schedule and wished owner "A.O.T." success. Thoms' advertisement in the *Havilah Courier*, January 4, 1868, indicated that it was arranged for on "nov 2" (1867).
18. *Havilah Courier*, May 16, 1868.
19. *Los Angeles News*, June 13, 1865.
20. *Ibid.*, June 15, 1866.
21. *Bancroft Scraps Set W 5, California Counties*, April 28, 1866 (May 5, 1866), 343; *Havilah Courier*, March 2, 1867.
22. *Los Angeles News*, June 13, 1865.
23. *Wilmington Journal*, October 14, 1865, in Benjamin I.

Hayes, *Scrapbooks*, no. 70, in the Bancroft Library.
24. *Los Angeles News*, January 12, 1866; *Havilah Courier*, April 27, 1867.
25. *Havilah Courier*, August 31, 1869; *Visalia Delta*, November 24, 1869.
26. *Inyo Independent*, August 8, 1870; *Visalia Delta*, August 10, 1870.
27. *Inyo Independent*, August 19, December 23, 1871.
28. *Ibid.*, May 20, 1871.
29. *Ibid.*, February 24, 1872.
30. *Ibid.*, March 23, 1872.
31. *Ibid.*, August 31, 1872.

CHAPTER VI

FROM ADVANCING RAILHEADS, STARTING IN THE SAN JOAQUIN AND SAN FERNANDO VALLEYS 1872-1876

"The stages from Allen's Camp for Los Angeles invariably go out crowded to their utmost capacity, and 'extras' are dispatched almost daily."
—Kern County Courier, May 8, 1875

CATTLEMEN, WHO depended upon the grasslands, were discouraging the settlement of the San Joaquin Valley, contended the *Visalia Delta* in July, 1869. They claimed that "not an acre in sixteen was fit for cultivation." Yet the forward-looking newspaper predicted that a growing farm populace would soon overwhelm these "bovine princes."[1] Besides the older farming community that had developed around Visalia, another one was evolving to the south along the lower reaches of the Kern River. In this latter farming area Bakersfield was emerging as the trading center on the so-called Kern Island.

Aware that Bakersfield, where he recently had established the *Kern County Courier*, was suffering from isolation, the editor in February, 1870, expressed the hope that the town soon would be on a stage line connecting Visalia and Los Angeles.[2] In April two Bakersfield businessmen, Horatio P. Livermore and Julius Chester, put a "comfortable wagon" on the road to White River, where a connection was made with the Telegraph Stage Company's line running between Visalia and the Kern River mines.³ A year later, in March, 1871, the proprietors provided stage service between Bakersfield and Visalia by way of a newly opened, nearly direct road. Within two weeks the *Kern County Courier* reported that the passenger and express business was rapidly increasing between these two towns.⁴

In May, 1871, George W. Andrews, whose stages had been running between Los Angeles and Havilah by way of the Tehachapi Valley, rerouted them through Fort Tejon and Bakersfield.⁵ Upon leaving the Tehachapi Mountains, his stages went directly northward over the plains by way of Hudson and Rosemyre's Ranch and Adobe Station. From Bakersfield they went southeast to the Baker grade, which afforded an easy, but winding, course up a ridge between Walker Basin and Caliente creeks to Walker Basin, where the stages turned northward to Havilah.

When southbound construction on the Southern Pacific Railroad reached Tipton, twenty miles south of Visalia, in July, 1872, the proprietors of the retreating Telegraph Stage Company developed plans to extend their operations to Los Angeles. They acquired Livermore and Chester's stages, which ran to Bakersfield. General manager Amos O. Thoms, by "almost superhuman exertions," inaugurated stage service to Los Angeles by way of Fort Tejon, Elizabeth Lake and San Fernando.⁶ While the company continued to send stages from Visalia to the Kern River mines by way of Linn's Valley, it also began to dispatch stages from Bakersfield by way of the Baker grade to Havilah, Kernville and Lone Pine.⁷

In July, 1873, Henry M. Newhall sold his interest in the Telegraph Stage Company to one of the state's most popular stagemen, William Hamilton, who shared the management of the firm with part-owner, William G. Roberts.⁸ A few months later the *Havilah Miner* reported that the town never had enjoyed "more general satisfaction in the regular delivery of the mails."⁹ An appreci-

Bakersfield businesses in the 1870s. (Courtesy, Kern County Museum)

ative traveler not only commended the company's courteous employees, but also praised the good rolling stock. There was no "epicurean spread" at the stations, but the passengers were "conveyed with celerity, safety, and cheapness."[10]

When the Telegraph Stage Company underwent a three-way division in June, 1874, the *Kern County Courier* explained that this was an outgrowth of the loss of mail contracts by William Hamilton and William G. Roberts. Their withdrawal was viewed with regret. Cyrus H. Cotter acquired the stages that connected the Southern Pacific railheads at Delano and San Fernando, which he operated as the Telegraph Stage Company. William Buckley became the owner of those running between Bakersfield and Lone Pine, while John Allman became the proprietor of those linking Visalia and Kernville.[11]

Southward construction on the Southern Pacific brought the railhead to Bakersfield in November, 1874, and by April, 1875, the trains were running to Caliente, at the foot of Tehachapi Pass. The companies whose stages had been departing from Bakersfield for a few months established connections at Caliente. Yet the *Kern County Courier* reported that Bakersfield's loss of two stage lines was being offset by the increasing general business activities.[12] From Caliente the Telegraph Stage Company's stages climbed a newly-constructed road along the course of Tehachapi Creek to the Tehachapi Valley, where they turned south over Oak Creek Pass. William Buckley's stages destined for Havilah and Lone Pine ascended a newly-built road to Walker Basin.

In the mid-1870s a trip between San Francisco and Los Angeles by way of the San Joaquin Valley was more costly than one aboard a coastal steamer, but the overland trip involved less travel time. In May, 1875, the *Kern County Courier* reported that the stages running between Caliente and San Fernando were "crowded to their utmost capacity," and extra coaches were being dispatched almost daily.[13] In September the Telegraph Stage Company began to acquire new "elegant Concord coaches."[14]

Even the most skillful stage drivers could not always avert accidents on their runs over the largely ungraded roads. While Hiram Meade was driving through the "hog wallows" south of Visalia in December, 1865, a lead bar broke and a horse became unruly. The reins were jerked from his hands, and the unmanaged team upset the stage. The driver's ankle was injured, and the passengers were shaken in the mishap.[15] When a stage toppled in Walker Basin in November, 1866, a passenger was injured by a splinter, while others suffered a broken leg and a fractured jaw.[16] Lewis Wood was driving through the "hog wallows" in January, 1867, when a king bolt broke. The fore wheels were torn away, and he was dragged from his seat. No passengers were injured, but Wood's jaw was broken.[17]

While Solomon S. Lefurgey was crossing the Greenhorn Mountains in April, 1869, his restless horses began to run downhill. The stage struck a rut, and he was bounced from his seat. A wheel ran over his arm, breaking it. The passengers stopped the entangled horses.[18] In April, 1873, a heavily-loaded stage upset near Havilah, resulting in severe injury to the driver, as well as bruises for several riders.[19] A Kern River ferryboat with a stage aboard was in midstream near Bakersfield in January, 1874, when the frightened horses pushed the vehicle backwards into the water. The passengers escaped from the tumbling stage, but a horse drowned.[20] A stage driver met a freight wagon on the Baker grade in August, 1874, and he asked the riders to alight before he attempted to pass. This precaution saved the passengers from probable injury, since the stage and horses tumbled down a steep hillside.[21] While a stage driver was descending toward Caliente in June, 1876, the line to the lead team broke, and the horses ran away. By holding the wheelers in check and applying the brakes, the driver regained control over the horses at the bottom of the grade. In the meantime several passengers had jumped from the stage, and one suffered a broken leg.[22]

For several days in January, 1866, a heavy snowfall prevented vehicular travel over the Greenhorn Mountains, and when the storm was over the stage proprietors were praised for their "grit and energy" in speedily restoring service.[23] Heavy snowfall again "laid an embargo upon travel" over these mountains in March, 1867.[24] In November, 1871, a sandstorm south of Bakersfield slowed a stage driver, and at the same time turned the countryside into a desert waste.[25] A sandstorm north of Willow Springs in December, 1875, stalled a stage driver for several hours.[26] In February, 1876, a heavy snowfall in Tehachapi Pass disrupted travel for several days.[27]

Simultaneously in July, 1876, the Southern Pacific Railroad Company completed the winding construction up Tehachapi Pass and a lengthy tunnel through the San Fernando Mountains.[28] While further railroad construction was underway between Mojave and Newhall by way of Lancaster and Palmdale, the Telegraph Stage Company continued to send its stages as usual by way of Willow Springs and Elizabeth Lake. These stage trips ceased upon the driving of the Southern Pacific's "last spike" at Lang's Station in Soledad Canyon in September, 1876, and a celebrated linking by railroad of San Francisco and Los Angeles.[29]

While the San Joaquin Valley's major stage lines were retreating before the expanding railroads in June, 1874, the editor of the *Mariposa Gazette* nostalgically recalled his long stage rides over the plains and "flying trips" in the mountains. Driven by careful drivers, the well-trained horses plodded along the roads, only to become "prancing steeds" as they approached a town. But "Alas!" the expanding railroads were wiping out the "long stage

Silver bullion on the Mojave Desert in 1876. (From George F. Weeks, California Copy)

routes."[30] By the mid-1870s the heyday of staging was over in the San Joaquin Valley, although the lore of stagecoaching became immortalized in the romantic history of the West.

NOTES

1. *Visalia Delta*, July 14, 1869.
2. *Kern County Courier*, February 8, 1870.
3. *Ibid.*, April 26, 1870.
4. *Ibid.*, March 18, April 1, 1871.
5. *Ibid.*, May 6, 1871.
6. *Ibid.*, June 29, July 13, 20, 1872; *Visalia Delta*, July 18, 1872.
7. *Ibid.*, August 3, 1872; *Visalia Delta*, February 6, March 27, 1873.
8. Benjamin I. Hayes, *Scrapbooks*, no. 109, in the Bancroft Library; *Inyo Independent*, July 12, 1873.
9. *Havilah Miner*, November 15, 1873.
10. *Sacramento Union*, November 22, 1873.
11. *Kern County Courier*, June 20, 1874.
12. *Ibid.*, May 1, 1875.
13. *Ibid.*, May 8, June 12, 1875.
14. *Inyo Independent*, September 25, 1875.
15. *Visalia Delta*, December 13, 1865.
16. *Ibid.*, November 28, 1866.
17. *Ibid.*, January 9, 1867.
18. *Ibid.*, April 14, 1869.
19. *Kern County Courier*, April 12, 1873.
20. *Ibid.*, January 10, 1874.
21. *Inyo Independent*, August 15, 1874.
22. *Courier-Californian*, June 15, 1876.
23. *Visalia Delta*, January 17, February 14, 1866.
24. *Ibid.*, April 3, 1867.
25. *Ibid.*, November 16, 1871.
26. *Kern County Gazette*, January 1, 1876.
27. *Kern County Courier*, February 5, 1876.
28. *Courier-Californian*, July 6, 20, 1876.
29. *Ibid.*, September 7, 1876.
30. *Mariposa Gazette*, July 3, 1874.

CHAPTER VII

STALKING THE STAGES: THE HOLDUP MEN, WHO WERE KNOWN AS "ROAD AGENTS" 1853-1876

"They 'sounded' the treasure box, but it giving back no sign, they dropped it, though . . . it contained a considerable amount."
—*Visalia Delta*, August 10, 1864

WHILE THE "honest miners' were busy extracting gold in the Sierra Nevada, robbers sometimes stalked the stage drivers who delivered the metallic wealth to the commercial centers of the state. Sought especially by these road agents were the express or treasure boxes entrusted to the drivers, but occasionally the passengers as well were compelled to surrender money, watches and other valuables. Some of these wide-ranging plunderers intercepted the stage drivers on the roads between Stockton and Sonora.

A Stockton-bound stage driver was waylaid in September, 1853, by road agents within a mile of Sonora, and they took an express box that belonged to Adams and Company. Subsequently much of the loot was recovered in the vicinity of the robbery, near Woods' Creek.[1] Upon reaching Stockton in January, 1876, a stage driver discovered that the two passengers had stolen the express of Wells, Fargo and Company. The box was opened with a chisel they had acquired during a short stay at Copperopolis.[2] In November, 1874, six masked men stopped a stage driver in the Salt Spring Valley between Milton and Sonora. The road agents stole a Wells, Fargo and Company express box, but they were unaware that there were two other boxes in the stage.[3]

In July, 1875, a masked gunman stopped a stage driver between Reynolds' Ferry and Copperopolis and demanded the express box. Investigating Wells, Fargo and Company agents found at the site an axe and the mangled box.[4] Eight years later the same road agent, who had long since become known as "Black Bart," again stopped a stage driver between Reynolds' Ferry and Copperopolis. At this twenty-eighth of his robberies, the notorious outlaw dropped a handkerchief, and the laundry mark led to his apprehension in San Francisco.[5] A robber who held up a stage driver between Sonora and Copperopolis in December, 1875, stole the Wells, Fargo and Company express box. A few days later he was captured by the sheriff of Calaveras County.[6]

With the beginning of the Civil War in April, 1861, it became apparent that many Confederate sympathizers were living at Snelling, Hornitos, Millerton and Visalia. They deplored the use of force to prevent the southern states from withdrawing from the Union. A businessman who dispatched money with the stage drivers asked one of them if he carried firearms. Asserting that he desired to be "neutral politically," the driver stated that he no longer carried weapons, since shooting of a robber "would be coercion with some folks."[7] Indeed, some outlawry in the San Joaquin Valley was guised as pro-South activity.

The notorious Mason and Henry gang ostensibly set out to organize and equip an army which would march to the aid of the Confederacy. Yet the *Visalia Delta* in July, 1865, characterized the gang's members as "infernal scoundrels" who roamed about intimidating, robbing and killing.[8] Presumably it was "Jeff. Davis' foragers," as the editor described them, who stopped a Gilroy-bound stage driver near Lone Willow in August, 1864.

"Black Bart" (Charles E. Boles). (Courtesy, California State Library)

Since the Wells, Fargo and Company express box did not rattle, the robbers wrongly assumed that it was empty, but they stole money from the passengers.[9] A greater degree of law and order prevailed with the ending of the Civil War.

Yet by the early 1870s road agents who stalked the stage drivers between Visalia and Gilroy were "displaying considerable activity." A driver was held up near Gilroy in August, 1870, by robbers who took the contents of the Wells, Fargo and Company express box.[10] An express box was stolen a month later by road agents who stopped a stage driver in that same area.[11] The notorious Tiburcio Vasquez, with two outlaw associates, intercepted a stage driver near Soap Lake east of Gilroy in August, 1871, and forced him to drive into a field out of sight from the road. A woman was allowed to remain in the stage, but the men were ordered to alight, and they were bound and robbed. The express box, concealed under the woman's dress, went undiscovered.[12] In November a stage driver was stopped in Pacheco Pass by road agents who took the contents of the express box.[13] Another driver who arrived at Firebaugh's Ferry in February, 1873, was met by two robbers and forced into the station. There other outlaws were holding the employees, and all the captives were robbed. In addition the express agent was forced to open a safe, and then the robbers rode away from the station with the plundered money and merchandise.[14]

Tiburcio Vasquez, who with two accomplices a few years earlier had intercepted a stage driver east of Gilroy, arrived with one associate at Freeman's Station near the eastern approach to Walker Pass. In a most daring robbery in February, 1874, Vasquez took captive stationkeeper Freeman S. Raymond and his wife, among others at the station, as well as the drivers and passengers of an arriving stage and two freight wagons. Besides seizing an express box, the robbers required the fourteen cap-

Tiburcio Vasquez. (Courtesy, California State Library)

tives to contribute to the "Vasquez fund." Moreover, they rode away with some of the best horses in the stable.[15]

In January, 1875, two masked men stopped a stage driver on the Baker grade southeast of Bakersfield and demanded the express box. Another stage driver was stopped in March in Walker Pass by two masked men. When the passengers realized what was happening, they dropped coins and watches to the floor. An express box surrendered by the driver contained no money, and subsequently the robbers were apprehended near Freeman's Station.[16]

Southbound construction on the Southern Pacific Railroad reached newly-founded Caliente at the southern end of the San Joaquin Valley in April, 1875. Caliente was a busy railhead for nearly a year while construction crews were at work in Tehachapi Pass. During its heyday the town, according to the *Kern County Gazette*, was overrun by "a horde of thieves and robbers" who comprised "the worst class of hoodlums in the country."[17]

The *Kern County Courier* observed that whenever there was a "stringency in the circulating medium" at Caliente, someone held up a stage driver and stole an express box. So frequent had these outrages become by the end of 1875, they caused only a slight sensation.[18] During an attempted robbery late in November two masked men stepped from behind rocks between Walker Basin and Caliente and ordered a stage driver to halt. He did not "heed the summons," and one of the road agents fired a gun, which caused the frightened horses to increase their speed and outrun the pursuers.[19] A few days later a stage driver was descending Tehachapi Pass toward Caliente when a robber ran in front of the horses and shouted, "Halt!" After the driver stopped the stage, he was ordered to throw down the express box. It was nighttime, and the driver could only see and hear one robber, but there may have been others in the vicinity.[20] Early in December a stage driver was approaching Cali-

Wanted poster for Richard Perkins, alias G. Brett Lytle, alias Dick Fellows, alias Robert Kirtland. (Courtesy, Wells Fargo Bank) ente when he was met by a road agent who demanded the express box.[21] A few days later a stage driver was stopped near Walker Basin by a masked robber who stepped in front of the horses. A pistol pointed at the driver persuaded him to surrender the express box.[22]

When a Kern County sheriff captured a horse thief in the Tehachapi Mountains in December, 1875, he discovered that the man possessed money stolen in a recent stage robbery. Taken into custody was a well-known outlaw, Richard Perkins, who also was known as G. Brett Lytle, Dick Fellows and Robert Kirtland. A few years earlier Perkins had been convicted of highway robbery, for which he was sentenced to the state prison. Because of good behavior his eight-year sentence had been cut short by a pardon in April, 1874. Following Perkins' conviction in Kern County, he escaped from the county jail, only to be recaptured within a week and delivered to the state prison.[23] Caliente's heyday ended in January, 1876, when it ceased to be the railhead, and the construction crews were moved higher in Tehachapi Pass. The town began to resemble the deserted mining towns of the early days.

Outlasting the menacing road agents were the names given some of their lurking places, notably that of Robbers' Roost. One Robbers' Roost was between Reynolds' Ferry and Copperopolis on Funk's Hill, where "Black Bart" committed the first of his admitted twenty-eight robberies. Another Robbers' Roost was located near the eastern approach to Walker Pass. This rock outcropping may have been the vantage point from which Tiburcio Vasquez and an accomplice planned their attack on Freeman's Station. The sandstone crags on a ridge between Soledad and Mint canyons in the mountains north of Los Angeles guarded the approach to Vasquez Canyon. The notorious outlaw spent some time near an outcropping there known as Robbers' Roost and Vasquez Rocks.

NOTES
1. *History of Tuolumne County, California*, 133-34, 267.
2. *Sonora Herald*, January 12, 1867.
3. *Union Democrat*, November 7, 1874.
4. *Ibid.*, July 31, 1875.
5. Joseph H. Jackson, *Bad Company*, 119-214, 334-35.
6. *Union Democrat*, December 4, 11, 1875.
7. *Mariposa Gazette*, as quoted in the *Visalia Delta*, June 20, 1861.
8. *Visalia Delta*, July 19, 1865.
9. *Ibid.*, August 10, 1864.
10. *Sacramento Union*, August 19, 1870.
11. *Ibid.*, September 19, 1870.
12. *Visalia Delta*, August 17, 1871.
13. *San Francisco Alta California*, November 17, 1871.
14. *Sacramento Union*, February 28, 1873.
15. *Inyo Independent*, February 28, 1874.
16. *Sacramento Union*, January 16, 1875; *Inyo Independent*, March 20, 27, 1875.
17. *Kern County Gazette*, December 4, 1875.
18. *Kern County Courier*, December 11, 1875.
19. *Ibid.*, December 4, 1875.
20. *Ibid.*
21. *Kern County Gazette*, December 11, 1875.
22. *Kern County Courier*, December 11, 1875.
23. *Kern County Gazette*, December 11, 1875, January 15, 22, 1876.

BIBLIOGRAPHY

BOOKS AND PAMPHLETS

Anonymous, *A History of Tuolumne County, California*. San Francisco: B. F. Alley, 1882.

Bell, Horace, *Reminiscences of a Ranger, or Early Times in Southern California*. Santa Barbara: Wallace Hebberd, 1927.

Brewer, William H., *Up and Down California in 1860-1864*. Berkeley and Los Angeles: University of California Press, 1966.

Buckbee, Edna B., *The Saga of Old Tuolumne*. New York: Press of the Pioneers, 1935.

Conkling, Roscoe P., and Conkling, Margaret B., *The Butterfield Overland Mail, 1857-1869*. Glendale: Arthur H. Clark Company, 1947.

Giffin, Helen S., and Woodward, Arthur, *The Story of El Tejon*. Los Angeles: Dawson's Book Shop, 1942.

Jackson, Joseph H., *Bad Company*. New York: Harcourt, Brace and Company, 1949.

Krythe, Mayme, *Port Admiral: Phineas Banning, 1830-1885*. San Francisco: California Historical Society, 1957.

Latta, Frank F., *El Camino Viejo a Los Angeles*. Bakersfield: Kern County Historical Society, 1936.

Ormsby, Waterman L., *The Butterfield Overland Mail*. San Marino: Huntington Library, 1955.

Outcalt, John, *A History of Merced County, California*. Los Angeles: Historic Record Company, 1925.

Paul, Rodman W., *California Gold: The Beginning of Mining in the Far West*. Cambridge: Harvard University Press, 1947.

Ripley, Vernette S., "The San Fernando Pass and the Pioneer Traffic that Went over It," *Historical Society of Southern California Quarterly*, XXX, no. 1 (March, 1948).

Smith, Wallace, *Garden of the Sun*. Fresno: California History Books, 1960.

Southern Pacific Bulletin, August, 1955. San Francisco: Southern Pacific Company, 1955.

Tinkham, George H., *History of San Joaquin County, California, with Biographical Sketches.* Los Angeles: Historic Record Company, 1923.

United States, War Department, *The War of the Rebellion: A Compilation of the Official Records of the Union and Confederate Armies.* Washington, D.C.: Government Printing Office, 1890-1901.

SCRAPBOOKS
Bancroft, Hubert H., *Bancroft scrapbooks* (Bancroft Library)
Hayes, Benjamin I., *Hayes scrapbooks* (Bancroft Library)

NEWSPAPERS

Bakersfield
  Courier-Californian
  Kern County Courier
  Kern County Gazette
Havilah
  Havilah Courier
  Havilah Miner
Independence
  Inyo Independent
Los Angeles
  Los Angeles News
  Los Angeles Star
Mariposa
  Mariposa Gazette
Millerton
  Fresno Expositor
Sacramento
  Sacramento Union
San Francisco
  San Francisco Alta California
Snelling
  San Joaquin Valley Argus
Sonora
  Sonora Herald
  Union Democrat
Stockton
  San Joaquin Republican
  Stockton Independent
Tuolumne City
  Tuolumne City News
Visalia
  Tulare County Record
  Visalia Delta

INDEX

A. N. Fisher and Company, 2, 4, 8, 9, 26, 28, 29
accidents, 10, 12, 22, 30-31, 38, 55-56
Adams and Company Express, 59
Alexander, David W., 16, 18, 20
Alexander and Banning stage company, 16, 18, 20
Allman, John, 54
Andrews, George W., 48, 52

Baker grade, 52, 55, 64
Bakersfield, 49, 51, 52, 53, 54, 55, 64
Banning, Phineas, 16, 18, 19, 20
Bear Valley, 2, 8
Bear Valley Road, 2, 8
Bennett, Patrick, 29, 30, 31
Bennett stage company, 29, 30
Big Oak Flat, 8
Birch, James E., 2
"Black Bart" (Charles E. Boles), 60, 61, 66
Brackman's Ferry, 29
Brickerhoff, Jacob W., 22
Brown, Samuel, 4
Buckley, William, 54
Butterfield, John, 18, 22

C. H. Sisson and Company, 6
Calaveras Grove, 8
Caliente, 54, 55, 64, 66
Caliente Creek, 44, 46, 52
California Stage Company, 2
Camp Independence, 45
Centerville, 29, 31
Central Pacific Railroad, 6, 8
Chester, Julius, 51, 52
Chinese Camp, 2, 6, 12
Chowchilla River, 31
Civil War, 4, 22, 28, 36, 45, 60, 62
Clarke, William H., 46
Clarke stage company, 46
Coast Line Stage Company, 36
Collister, John, 48
Converse's Ferry, 16
Copperopolis, 6, 59, 60, 66
Coso Range, 21, 26, 43
Cotter, Cyrus H., 54
Coulterville, 8

Cox's Ferry, 10
Cross Creek, 38

Davis, Israel W., 29, 45, 46
Davis stage company, 29, 45, 46
Delano, 54
Desert Springs, 48
Diablo Range, 20-21
Dickenson's Ferry, 2
Dillon, John, 2
Dillon and Company, 2, 4
Dinsmore, William B., 22
Dooley, Maurice J., 2, 4, 6
Dooley and Company, 4, 6
Dowst, Wesley B., 10
drivers (stage), 1, 8, 10, 12, 22, 28, 29, 31, 38, 40, 41, 46, 55, 56, 59, 60, 62, 64, 66

El Camino Viejo, 15
Elizabeth Lake, 15, 16, 46, 52, 56
Ellison, James A., 4, 6, 8
Ellison and Company, 4, 6, 8
Evans, Lt. Col. George S., 45
express, 1, 4, 25, 26, 31, 40, 44, 45, 52, 59, 60, 62, 64, 66

farming, 9, 35, 51
Fellows, Dick. See Perkins, Richard
ferries, 1, 2, 6, 8, 10, 12, 16, 20, 29, 31, 35, 38, 40, 55, 60, 62, 66
Firebaugh's Ferry, 20, 31, 35, 38, 40, 62
Fisher, Alvin N., 2, 9
Fisher, Samuel, 2, 9, 10
Fisher, Zenas, 9, 10
Fisher and Company, 8, 10
Fleming, Russell H., 31
Fort Tejon, 15, 16, 20, 21, 22, 49, 52
Fountain Springs, 44
Freeman's Station, 62, 64, 66
freighting, 16, 18, 43, 44
Fresno, 31, 41
Fresno Slough, 38

Gardner, T. N. ("Old Honesty"), 10, 12
George, Daniel, 41
Gilroy, 15, 21, 29, 35, 36, 40, 41, 62
gold rush (California), 1, 4, 8, 15, 16
gold rush (Kern River), 18, 25

Gordon, Peter, 12
Gordon's Ferry, 16, 20
Goshen, 41
Greenhorn Mountains, 44, 45, 55, 56
Hamilton, William, 52, 54
Harper, Samuel, 48
Havilah, 36, 45, 46, 47, 48, 49, 52, 54, 55
Heath and Emory's Ferry, 2
Heston, Thomas M., 25, 26, 31, 44
Heston express, 25
Heston stage company, 25-26
Hice, William L., 26, 28, 31
Hice and Wilson stage company, 26, 28, 44
Hice stage company, 26, 28
Hornitos, 2, 8, 9, 10, 11, 12, 25, 26, 28, 29, 30, 31, 44, 60

Indians, 16, 18, 22, 35, 44-45

Jamestown, 2
Jones' Ferry, 31

Kaweah River, 16
Kelty, Eugene C., 2, 4
Kelty and Reynolds stage company, 2, 4
Kern River, 16, 18, 20, 25, 36, 43, 44, 45, 51, 52, 55
Kernville, 36, 45, 48, 52, 54
Keyesville, 18, 25, 44, 45
Kings River, 16, 20, 26, 29, 30, 38, 40
Kinson, Victor, 22
Kinyon, Marcus L., 20
Knight's Ferry, 1, 6, 10, 12

Lang's Station, 56
Lathrop, 6, 10
Lefurgey, Solomon S., 40, 55
Linn's Valley, 36, 44, 45, 52
Livermore, Horatio P., 51, 52
Livermore and Chester stage company, 51, 52
Lone Pine, 43, 48, 49, 52, 54
Lone Willow, 60
Los Angeles, 15, 16, 18, 20, 21, 22, 28, 43, 44, 46, 48, 49, 51, 52, 54, 56, 66
Los Angeles and Keyesville Road, 44
Los Angeles and Stockton Road, 16, 26, 28, 44, 46
Lytle, G. Brett. See Perkins, Richard

McCloud, Alonzo, 2
McFarlane Road, 45
mail, 1, 2, 4, 6, 8-9, 10, 12, 18, 25, 28, 29, 30, 31, 36, 38, 40, 44, 45, 48, 49, 52, 54
Mariposa, 2, 4, 7, 8, 9, 10, 12, 25, 26
Mariposa Creek, 12, 30, 31
Mariposa Road, 2, 8, 10
Mason and Henry gang, 60
Meade, Hiram, 45, 46, 55
Meade and Clarke stage company, 46
Meade and Davis stage company, 45-46
Merced, 10, 31, 41
Merced Falls, 2
Merced River, 1, 2, 4, 9, 10, 16
Millerton, 9, 25, 26, 27, 28, 29, 30, 31, 36, 60
Milton, 6, 60
mining, 1, 4, 8, 15, 18, 21, 25, 26, 28, 29, 35, 43, 44, 45, 48, 52
Modesto, 10, 30
Mojave, 56
Mojave Plains, 15, 46, 57
Mono Lake, 21, 26, 43
Morse, Charles, 12
Mott, Simeon H., 12

Newhall, 56
Newhall, Henry M., 39, 41, 48, 52

Oak Creek Pass, 46, 54
O'Byrne's Ferry, 8
Overland Mail Company, 18, 20, 21, 22, 26, 28, 35, 36
Owens Valley, 21, 26, 35, 44, 45, 48
Owens Valley Stage Line, 45

Pacheco Creek, 38, 40
Pacheco Pass, 20, 26, 40, 62
Paradise City, 9, 30
People's Accommodation and Express Company, 6
Perkins, Richard, 65, 66
Peters, 6
Phillips' Ferry, 16
Poole's Ferry, 16

INDEX

railroads, 6, 8, 10, 13, 30, 31, 36, 40 41, 51, 52, 54, 56, 64, 66
ranching, 9, 15, 18, 45, 51
Raymond, Freeman S., 45, 62
Red Banks, 30
Red Bird Line, 2
Reynolds, Gilbert C., 2, 4
Reynolds' Ferry, 8, 60, 66
Rice, Charles, 45
Rice and Raymond stage company, 45
roads, 1, 2, 8, 10, 15, 16, 18, 20-21, 25-26, 28, 38, 40, 43-44, 45, 46, 52, 54, 55
robberies, 59, 60, 62, 64, 66
Robbers' Roost, 66
Roberts, William G., 41, 52, 54
Robinson, Henry W., 48
Robinson stage company, 48-49

S. and Z. Fisher's Stage Company, 8, 9, 10, 30
Sacramento, 4, 6
Salt Springs Valley, 59
San Emigdio Pass, 15
San Fernando, 16, 52, 54
San Fernando Mountains, 15, 16, 20 56
San Fernando Valley, 51
San Francisco, 15, 18, 20, 21, 26, 30, 36, 43, 46, 48, 54, 56, 60
San Francisco and San Jose Railroad, 36, 41
San Francisco Bay, 6, 36
San Francisquito Canyon, 15
San Joaquin River, 1, 16, 20, 26, 29, 31
San Joaquin Valley, 1, 15, 20, 22, 28, 35, 38, 48, 51, 54, 56, 58, 60, 64
San Joaquin Valley Railroad, 6, 10, 30, 31, 41
San Jose, 15, 21, 35, 36, 40, 46
San Pedro, 16, 18
Santa Clara and Pajaro Valley Railroad, 40, 41
Schleigh, Charles H., 45
Scottsburg, 25, 26, 29
Second Cavalry, California Volunteers, 45
Sheep Camp, 30
Sierra Nevada, 1, 8, 16, 18, 21, 25, 35, 43, 44, 48, 59
Silman, Lemuel H., 9, 10, 30
Sinks of the Tejon, 20
Sisson, Charles H., 6

Sisson and Company Stage Line, 6
Slate Range, 44
Smith, David, 18
Smith's Ferry, 16, 29, 38
Snediker, James L., 12
Snelling, 2, 9, 30, 36, 60
Snelling Road, 10
Soap Lake, 62
Sonora, 2, 4, 5, 6, 8, 10, 12, 59, 60
Sonora Road, 1-2, 4, 8, 10
Southern Pacific Railroad, 41, 52, 54, 56, 64
stagecoaches, 1, 2, 12, 16, 21, 25, 26, 29, 36, 41, 46, 51, 55
Stanislaus River, 1, 2, 4, 8, 10
Stockton, 1, 2, 3, 4, 6, 9, 10, 12, 13, 15, 26, 28, 30, 59
Stockton and Copperopolis Railroad, 6
storms, 10, 12, 21, 22, 23, 29, 35, 38, 40, 44, 56

Tehachapi Creek, 54
Tehachapi Mountains, 15, 52, 66
Tehachapi Pass, 54, 56, 64, 66
Tehachapi Valley, 46, 52, 54
Tejon Indian Reservation, 16, 18
Tejon Pass ("Old"), 15
Tejon Pass ("New"), 15
Telegraph Stage Company, 29, 31, 36, 38, 40, 41, 46, 48-49, 51, 52, 54, 55, 56
Thoms, Amos O., 26, 28, 29, 34, 36, 38, 40, 41, 46, 48, 52
Tipton (California), 52
Tipton (Missouri), 20
Tollgate Canyon, 46
Tomlinson, John J., 46, 48
Tomlinson Stage Company, 46, 48
tourists, 8
Tuolumne City, 9, 30
Tuolumne River, 1, 2, 4, 9, 10, 16, 30

Union Post Office, 29

Vasquez, Tiburcio, 62, 63, 64, 66
Vasquez Canyon, 66
Visalia, 9, 15, 18, 20, 21, 22, 25, 26, 28, 29, 30, 31, 35, 36, 37, 38, 40, 41, 43, 44, 45, 46, 49, 51, 52, 54, 55, 60, 62

Walker Basin, 44, 45, 46, 52, 54, 55, 64, 66
Walker Pass, 43, 44, 48, 62, 64, 66
Wells, Fargo and Company Express, 59, 60, 62
White, James C., 45
White River, 51
Whitmore's Ferry, 20, 35, 38
Willow Springs, 46, 56
Wilson, Charles, 18
Wilson, John, 28, 44
Wilson and Young stage company, 44
Winslow, Aseal, 22, 28
Wood, Lewis, 55

Yosemite Valley, 8
Young, John A., 44

NEW ARRANGEMENT!
A. N. FISHER & CO.'S
Stage Line,
FOR STOCKTON.

From and after MAY 3d the Stage will leave Mariposa, ON ALTERNATE DAYS, AT 1 O'CLOCK, P. M.

Via the New Bear Valley Road,
....Connecting with....

BEAR VALLEY, MOUNT OPHIR, QUARTZBURG, HORNITAS, MURRAY'S BRIDGE, SNELLINGS, DICKINSON'S AND HEATH & EMORY'S FERRIES

N. B. Passengers for French Bar, Knight's Ferry or Sonora, will take A. N. Fisher & Co.'s Stage at Hornitas.

Office at Wells, Fargo & Co.'s Main st., Mariposa

J. B. CONDON, Agent.

☞ The above Line connects at Hornitos with the Visalia stage, for Millerton, King's River and Visalia.   27-tf

---

U. S. MAIL STAGE.

Telegraph Line!
FROM SAN JOSE TO VISALIA.

ON AND AFTER MARCH 31, 1865, STAGES will leave San Jose every **Monday** and **Thursday**, on the arrival of the 8 o'clock train, from San Francisco, for

LONE WILLOW,
FIREBAUGH'S FERRY,
FRESNO CITY,
KINGS RIVER and VISALIA.

Return Stages leave Visalia **Tuesday** and **Friday**, at 6 o'clock, A. M.

Connecting at Visalia with Stage for

TULE RIVER,
WHITE RIVER,
LINN'S VALLEY,
KERN RIVER,
and the CLEAR CREEK MINES.

A. O. THOMS,........Proprietor.

Visalia, April 12, 1865.   ap12-tf.

---

426   STATE REGISTER.   [1859.

OVERLAND MAIL COMPANY,
VIA LOS ANGELES.
TIME OF DEPARTURE CHANGED

On and after the first day of December, 1858, the Coaches of THE OVERLAND MAIL COMPANY will leave the Office,

CORNER of WASHINGTON and KEARNY STS.
(PLAZA,) as follows:

THROUGH MAIL,

MONDAY AND FRIDAY, at 12 o'clock, M.

Fort Yuma and Intermediate Stations,

MONDAY, WEDNESDAY AND FRIDAY,

At 12 o'clock, MERIDIAN, instead of 12 o'clock, Midnight, as heretofore.

FARE—FROM SAN FRANCISCO TO FORT SMITH, ARKANSAS, OR TO TERMINUS OF THE PACIFIC RAILROAD,

☞ **ONE HUNDRED DOLLARS!** ☜

LOUIS McLANE, Agent Overland Mail Co.

TO OUR AGENTS:

We have e...
Matter for those C...
Our charges from...
Freight to...
Valuables...
Freight to...
Valuables,...
Freight to...

No package will...
on this route.